I0048693

Piercing the Corporate Veil

Making British companies work for us all

Derek Hammersley

HEDDON PUBLISHING

First published in the United Kingdom 2025 by Heddon Publishing

www.heddonpublishing.com

Copyright © Derek Hammersley 2025
The right of Derek Hammersley to be identified as the author of this work has been
asserted by him in accordance with the Copyright, Designs and Patents Act 1988.

A catalogue record for this book is available from the British Library

ISBN
(hardback) 978-1-917824-07-1
(paperback) 978-1-917824-08-8
(ebook) 978-1-917824-09-5

All rights reserved. No part of this publication may be reproduced, stored in a retrieval
system or transmitted in any form or by any means, electric, mechanical, photocopying,
recording or otherwise, without the prior permission of the publisher.

This publication is designed to provide accurate and authoritative information in regard
to the subject matter covered. While the publisher and author have used their best
efforts in preparing this book, they make no representations or warranties with respect
to the accuracy or completeness of the contents of this book.

Cover Design: Catherine Clarke Design

For Janet, Claire, John, Laura, Robert and Joseph
and Isabella with love.

CONTENTS

The Global Perspective

The Future

Introduction

"The first truth is that the liberty of a democracy is not safe if the people tolerate the growth of private power to a point where it becomes stronger than their democratic state itself. That, in its essence, is fascism – ownership of government by an individual, by a group, or by any other controlling private power... Among us today a concentration of private power without equal in history is growing."

Franklin D. Roosevelt (1930s)

In our democratic, liberal society, where universal suffrage means we all have the right to vote, and where we have access to so much information and a good understanding of society, both locally and internationally, we nevertheless come up against some limitations and threats which seem to be out of our hands. Faced with an increasingly complex network of businesses with complicated structures which many of us would struggle to make sense of, we can see that such businesses have a detrimental effect on our lives and yet feel powerless to change this.

Through this book I intend to show how and why this has happened in the UK, as well as why it is being allowed to continue. My aim is to create a greater understanding of the current situation while also helping to develop some alternative solutions, to facilitate taking some of this control away from the faceless corporations and placing it back in the hands of its rightful owners, the citizens of Britain.

For the past four decades, politicians and economists have trained their sights on the world of business and finance, agonising over the assumed effects of globalisation on Britain's economy and social fabric.

Globalisation has three major roots: first, the unprecedented growth in containerised sea transport capacity starting in 1960 and accelerating exponentially from the 1980s and 1990s; second, the availability and universal use of the easily created and liquidated limited liability company in most countries of the world; finally, the lifting of exchange controls in the 1980s, enabling a web of interlinked companies to move funds and assets at will around the world. This is what people mean when they use the catch-all term 'globalisation' today.

Often, the global nature of business can give the impression that it is too large for a state to contain or control, taking the problem out of any one government's hands. Scanning the horizon through the globalisation telescope, politicians and economists alike have failed to recognise that the damage is homegrown.

The war in Ukraine has shown the immense power of states to quickly curb the activities of companies, which contrasts starkly with the UK's apparent inability to control them at home, at even the most basic level. This despite the near constant but brief outrage and one-day headlines following the relentless stream of corporate failure in the UK and the resulting damage to the elderly and the disadvantaged, to pensions and to the state's funding. We are aware of the apparent extensive oversight by regulatory bodies, which appear ineffective, and supposedly stiffer penalties that are almost never applied.

We as citizens could be forgiven for wanting to look the other way. The problem seems too wide-reaching, and the scale can make it seem incomprehensible.

It is understandable that people feel powerless in the face of business, especially in a global marketplace. It can be easy to shrug our shoulders and think there is nothing we can do; it is all out of our hands, and sometimes above our heads. But we are affected every day of our lives by the effects of an antiquated company law.

The current legal situation dates to the 19th century and is not fitting for today's world. It is of vital importance that citizens understand its significance and how it affects them directly when it is often supposed to be entirely separate to general, societal and criminal law. The company is treated as a citizen in its own right yet is not held accountable in the same way individual citizens are.

Throughout the course of this this book I will set out the arguments for why and how company law needs to change, so that it is no longer protecting only the shareholders of an organisation but all who are affected by that company's practices, whether consumers, clients, employees, contractors, suppliers, or the state.

To date this has never been done, because those whose interests are best served by the current structures have little incentive to make changes – why would they, when the present situation is so beneficial to them? And although in recent decades the company has been identified as a major contributing factor to the failure of governments meeting the economic expectations of their citizens, no-one has proposed changing company law, how it functions, or suggesting how this might be done. Nor have they made the link that making these changes could reverse the transfer of power to companies.

A radical rewrite of company law is not a black or white situation, where damage is done to one section of society for the benefit of another. However, it is necessary to identify where the current state of affairs falls down, in terms of allocating risk away from the company and placing it with the citizen. That cannot be right.

In rewriting the law we would look to move the associated risks in terms of company activity where they belong, with the investor/speculator.

But the aim in creating new legislation would not be to damage any company or limit world (or other) trade. In removing the ability of companies to damage society by ensuring that they obey the law, it will also be necessary to put in place legislation to ensure this does not inhibit them from trading successfully and profitably.

Were we coming at this task afresh, it is extremely unlikely that we would develop the company structure we presently use, inherited from the Victorians.

So how can this situation be brought up-to-date and any necessary changes made? By presenting a valid, modern alternative, which removes or reverses the potentially dangerous wrong-turnings of the past and puts power back where it was not always intended, but where it should be: with the citizen.

What is a limited company?

It is not always helpful to ask in the abstract: 'What is a limited liability company?' It may be better to ask, 'What does a company do?', 'How does a company work?', or 'For whom does a company work?' You could also ask, 'Why would somebody create a company?'

A very simple, straightforward example is required in response.

You, John Smith, have had a brilliant idea for a business venture, guaranteed to make money. As in all business ventures, there are risks. Since you have considerable wealth and no wish to jeopardise this, you decide to pursue the venture using a limited liability company (LLC). This will offer you and your finances protection.

To go about setting up an LLC in the UK, you would make use of the Companies Act 2006. You set up your company with 100 shares of £1, of which you pay two shares up in cash. Shares serve three functions: they indicate ownership (or partial ownership) of a company; they are a means to raise capital for a business, and they give the shareholders votes by which they exercise collective control over the running of a company. There is no legal requirement to pay for shares issued at this stage but, having opened a bank account, a small balance may be required. You still owe the company £98 for the remaining shares.

You will have to decide on a name for your new company, so you imaginatively select John Smith Limited. The staff at Companies House, which is tasked with recording new companies, will record your new company details and give you a certificate of incorporation. This can be used to enable a bank to set up everything necessary for the new company to use their facilities. You, John Smith, are recorded at Companies House as the sole director of John Smith Limited (we will look much later at what 'director' means) and the sole shareholder (owner), with two £1 shares.

John Smith Limited is a piece of paper, with a bank account which contains £2.

Your business idea involves buying and selling a specialised piece of machinery. You register the company with His Majesty's Revenue & Customs for Corporation Tax (we will ignore VAT for the sake of simplicity). The state has recognised the company name as distinct from your own.

You decide to loan the company £100,000 so you write a loan agreement which you sign in person as John Smith, director of John Smith Limited. The company now has £100,002 in the bank and owes you £100,000.

You make a contract on behalf of the company with XYZ Limited to buy a machine for £60,000, and sign it on behalf of the company.

You make another contract with ABC Limited to sell the machine for £120,000, and sign it on behalf of the company.

The sale proceeds successfully.

The company now has £160,002 in the bank, of which £100,000 is owed to you under the loan agreement and £60,002 belongs to the company, not to you directly.

You pay your corporation tax of £12,000 on the £60,000 profit (assuming a rate of 20%), leaving the company with £148,002.

As John Smith, the sole shareholder, you instruct John Smith, the director, to authorise John Smith Limited to pay out to the sole shareholder (i.e. you) a dividend of £48,000. You also demand repayment of the loan of £100,000.

We are now back at the beginning, with John Smith Limited having £2 in the bank.

Any legal liability arising from the business transaction is the responsibility of the company, up to a maximum of the capital of £100, in this case including the £98 of the share capital still unpaid.

In the event of a legal claim against John Smith Ltd, this can be made against the company, but as it has no assets (money), any damages could only be paid up to a maximum of £100. On very rare occasions, in the event of major criminal fraud, courts have looked to shareholders and directors for recovery, but this is extremely rare.

It does not take a great deal of imagination or legal knowledge to see how this simple example answers the initial questions: 'What does a company do?', 'How does a company work?', 'For whom does a company work?' and 'Why would you create a company?'

The principle does not change if you multiply the number of shareholders by 1000, the number of directors by ten, or the value of the transaction by 1,000,000. An LLC limits the liability of its investors to the amount of their initial investment. It is clearly in their financial interest to set up an LLC and reduce their business risk.

What should this lead us to conclude at this stage?

Firstly, John Smith could have transacted his business as an individual, formed a partnership, an unincorporated association, or an unlimited company. Forming an LLC to carry out this transaction was one of many ways of carrying on business, and a relatively new one. LLCs do not equate to 'markets' or 'the market', or 'free markets'.

Secondly, in forming a company, any equating of the company to an entity in its own right is pure sophistry. When one or more individuals form a company, they buy a name with which they can contract the buying and selling of goods and services and which the state, through law, recognises. Once the name of the company is on a piece of paper, all the human beings involved could open bank accounts, employ other people, sign contracts, and carry on trade in that name. In the John Smith Ltd example, the formation of the company is the act of only one person, which enables every other human participant to act either officially or through a contractual relationship. The company only exists to the extent that use is made of it by human action and reaction. It is no more than a name on a piece of paper.

A Brief History of the Limited Liability Company in Britain

The outline of company law as we know it today was fixed in the mid-19th century by a small group of peers (in the House of Lords), their parliamentary supporters, and the commercial middle class who had, or controlled, the vote, in order to meet their requirement for limiting the liability on their investments. The intention was to encourage investment by other members of this small group at a time of rapid expansion in industry and railway development, and also at a time when only a small percentage of the adult population had a vote.

"The Companies Act of 1862, following on from the Companies Act of 1855, being the culmination of a series of changes removing all obstacles to incorporation."[1]

Indeed, in just six years' time, English lawmakers eliminated virtually all constraints: Britain went from a system of tight restrictions to one of the most permissive in Europe. Although the Act of 1855 was the defining break with the earlier British government view on limited liability

---

[1] The Impact of the Companies Act of 1862 Extending Limited Liability to the Banking and Financial Sector in the English Crisis of 1866. David Foucaud in Revue économique Volume 62, Issue 5, 2011, pages 867 to 897

companies, it was the Companies Act of 1862 which defined the future direction and format for later companies acts, up to and including that of 2006.

Following the abolition of slavery in 1833, the capital available in the hands of the aristocracy and middle class was added to by the largest distribution of state funds ever made. Rather than compensate the slaves, the government chose to compensate the slave-owners, on an unprecedented scale, distributing in today's money £17 billion, 40% of the national budget, to 3000 families.

This vast disparity of wealth meant that capital was concentrated into few hands and there were many capitalists looking to invest in the future businesses of the country without wishing to join in the running of those businesses. A commercial mechanism to enable capitalists to come together for commercial purposes and to limit their liability at the outset of the venture appeared at the right time.

Implemented in November 1862, the Companies Acts reformed the nature of companies: by meeting certain simple conditions and filing their Articles of Association, any company was recognised as a legal entity, consisting of unlimited transferable shares, and let shareholders benefit from limited liability. This law did not affect companies with fewer than seven shareholders, which kept their former status. Companies with eight to twenty shareholders were able to choose their system, while those with more than twenty shareholders had to adopt limited liability status.

"Between 1856 and 1862, the 2,500 limited-liability companies established absorbed 30 million pounds, whereas for the 1863-1866 period the number of declarations filed was about 3,500 for an amount of 650 million pounds."[2]

---

[2] Anthony Pulbrook, The Companies Act, 1862

In 1897, the House of Lords – overturning the earlier decisions of lower courts – confirmed that a limited liability company had a separate legal identity to its founder. Mr Salomon was the name of the person who founded the company. His new, invisible, companion was called Salomon and Co Ltd.

Between 1862 and 1948, company law changed little in content, and almost not at all in intent. The major reviews occurred in 1908, 1928 and 1948.

1928 Britain was a different country to the one of 1908. A bloody and expensive war from 1914 to 1918 had radically changed its economic and political outline. The Act of 1928 coincided with the Representation of the People Act (Equal Franchise), whereby women under the age of thirty were given the right to vote and Britain finally became a democracy. Women over thirty had been enfranchised by the Representation of the People Act 1918, which abolished all property qualifications for men and enfranchised women over thirty, subject to a property qualification.

By 1948, the outlook was quite different again. Britain was virtually bankrupt following the Second World War, struggling to untangle itself from some of its major colonies. It had a Labour government which had been elected to undertake major political and economic change and was in the process of doing so. The most likely reason why changes to Company Law in 1948 were so limited was that the Cohen Committee, tasked with proposing amendments, was set up in 1943, during the war and under a government of national unity. The committee was staffed by the same circle that traditionally carried out such reviews and, more importantly, the postwar government was beset by challenges it considered of greater importance.

The 1948 Act was a step forward in Company Law but did not deviate from the basic premise of protecting investors and, to some extent, creditors, and was still based soundly on the principles of the 1855/1862 Acts.

After joining the EU (EEC) in 1973, EU company law directives had to be incorporated into British Company Law and represented a departure from the traditional approach. The last major revision of company law took place in 2006.

The Companies Act 2006 is said to be the largest piece of legislation ever passed by Parliament, with 1300 sections and sixteen schedules, but it contained no substantive new measures, other than the continued deregulation of private companies.

The 2006 Act is in substance a 19th century document modestly updated in limited areas by the requirements of the European Union. This is the Act which we will consider in greater detail in this book.

Where we are now

Chapter 1
Globalisation

Before looking in detail at the situation in Britain, we should review the global environment in which British business operates and how this may develop in the future.

World trade in goods expanded rapidly from the 1980s onwards but in terms of total world GDP it is still small, and the volume of funds needed to finance world trade in goods and services is equally modest. These sums are dwarfed by those flowing worldwide between companies, in particular finance companies and banks, for purposes other than funding trading activity. The critical factor was the facility to create a worldwide web of related companies, all owning and controlling assets and people with the immense benefit that each is a discrete legal entity which can be grown or discarded as necessary with, in theory, no risk. The exceptions to this are so rare that they prove the rule.

Volumes of academic work have looked to define the concept of globalisation, the results dependent very much on the theory of global politics espoused by the writer. Realism (encompassing classical realism, neorealism, and possibly post-realism), liberalism, neo-liberalism and Marxism (encompassing neo-Marxism and critical theory) can all be considered as 'worldviews', and colour any analysis and explanation.

The starting point of an examination of a concept can often decide the end point. The debate in respect of 'globalisation' over the last twenty or thirty years has generally started with markets. Economists love markets as a catch-all term, usually to avoid having to delve deeply into legal and political details.

Professor Rodrik, one of the most thoughtful analysers of this concept, says: "International markets operate outside the formal institutional framework of sovereign entities and therefore, absent special arrangements, are deprived of the support of those frameworks. Equally important, international markets operate across the institutional boundaries demarcating states and their jurisdictions. These two facts, – the absence of an overall framework for global markets and the tensions such markets generate between local institutions – are fundamental to understanding economic globalization."[3]

So far so good, but which markets: the market for soya beans, deck cranes, derivatives, currencies, cheap clothing, insurance…? The list goes on for page after page. Are these markets all the same? Clearly not. So what, if anything, is a common factor underlying almost all trade in these hundreds or thousands of markets? The answer is that they are almost without exception carried on through the medium of a limited liability company and also, almost without exception, a company which is part of an international group of companies.

International groups of companies have operated for well over a century, long before the term 'globalisation' became fashionable. What is new is that the oversight over these companies and groups of companies has been drastically reduced and this, combined with the lifting of exchange

---

[3] The Globalization Paradox, Dani Rodrik, Oxford University Press, 2011

controls, has handed unimaginable levels of power and influence to them.

As a rule, countries do not trade with each other; businesses do. And of these businesses the vast majority are groups of companies interlocking but located in many different countries and incorporated under the legal code of the host country. This turns what on the face of it is a monolithic structure into a disparate and far looser one. It would be more exact to refer not to multinational or transnational companies but rather to a group of local national companies linked to one holding company through share ownership, with potentially differing levels of ownership. This is easier to deal with, and less threatening.

International Trade Today

The term globalisation is used today in a way which suggests that the 195 states in the world are frantically trading with each other. This is not the case. World Trade Organization statistics tell us that the top ten exporter countries of manufactures in 2017 represented 84% of all trade, and a quick calculation also reveals that the top five represented 75% of all trade. The list of countries brings no surprises. (Fig.1)

The share for the EU is derived from combining the external exports of its member states (e.g., Germany 7.1%, Netherlands 3.9%, Italy 2.8%, France 2.7%, etc.) and is distinct from the 14.3% figure for extra-EU exports (that is exports leaving the EU which ,if substituted, would give a different overall percentage share) as reported by Eurostat in some sources, as the latter is a different calculation method. When individual EU countries are in the top 10 list, the total for the top 10 unique entities/blocs will be around 84%.

The comparable figures for 2023 would be the top ten world exporting blocs at 80 % and importing 68%. As expected, the top ten major export and import nations have reduced their shares but not by much.

In using these statistics, it is correct to include intra-European Union trade as this must be included to show how little trade flows outside these major trading nations and how rapidly trade volumes decrease once outside the top five trading nations (or, better, blocks).

It is illuminating to note that China, the United States and Germany account for 30% of world merchandise trade. For completeness, the equivalent figures for imports are 70% of world GDP for the top ten importing nations and 59% for the top five. (Fig. 2)

	%
European Union (28)	38.9 (European Union extra-EU exports 14.3%)
China	17.8
United States of America	9.4
Japan	5.0
Korea, Republic of	4.3
Mexico	2.8
Singapore	2.3
Chinese Taipei (Taiwan)	2.2
Canada	1.7
Total	**84.4**

Figure 1

	%
European Union	32.8 (European Union extra-EU imports 10.6%)
United States of America	14.1
China	8.9
Hong Kong, China	0.3
Japan	3.1
Canada	2.6
Mexico	2.5
Korea, Republic of	2.3
India	1.7
Singapore	1.7
Total	**70.0**

Figure 2

What these figures show is that, far from being universal, world merchandise trade is concentrated into large volumes of exchange between a few major countries or, in the case of the European Union, trade blocks. They also clearly show the major trade imbalances which cause the recurring flare-ups of trade disputes and wars between these major trading nations and blocks.

At this point it may be useful to expand on the considerable difference between what the world understands as globalisation and what constitutes turbo-capitalism, and to consider whether the former must always lead to a breakdown in the implicit social contract which arises when the citizen, through the state, allows limited liability for large-scale business activities. Equally, must it also result in the ending of the post-Second World War social contract in Europe which led to the social market economy?

The post-1945 consensus began to break down in some countries in the 1980s as exchange controls were removed and Asian economies opened up, but not everywhere. Most responsible European, and some United States, companies expanded into Asia; mainly China at this time, but did not reduce local production or employment terms. Seeing the potential markets in Asia and its then lack of production capacity and expertise, they moved obsolete (for Europe or the United States) capacity to Asia and began production. Many German companies, including BMW and Volkswagen, led this move, as well as developing production in such countries as Brazil and Mexico. There was considerable logic in this development at this time; it is only necessary to look at, for example, car production statistics (Fig.3) for these countries today to see that home (European) production could never have supplied or even been accepted by the countries concerned.

Today Volkswagen has 119 production facilities in nineteen European countries and ten in Asia, Africa and the

Americas. BMW has a smaller footprint but produces in Germany, China, Mexico, the United States, India and South Africa. From an Asian perspective, Toyota produces in twenty-six countries including the United Kingdom, as does Nissan and formerly, pre-Brexit, Honda.

All these companies have major production facilities in their home countries; indeed, the Wolfsburg facility of Volkswagen can claim to be the largest in the world. These companies, along with many others, did not break the social contract, although to what extent they may have done without supporting legislation is an open question.

We should suppose that responsible, professionally managed and successful companies accept that to do business in modern democracies they will have to accept limitations on some activity and controls on employment, together with a reasonable level of taxation, to fund the social infrastructure from which they benefit.

It can be argued that this level of globalisation has benefited many developing countries whilst not materially harming the home country. The examples I've given are from Germany and Japan but one could also add other European countries and perhaps a few United States companies.

Top 10 Car Producing Countries in the World (OICA 2021)

Country	Volume Million
China	26.08
United States	9.17
Japan	7.85
India	4.40
South Korea	3.46
Germany	3.31
Mexico	3.15
Brazil	2.25

Figure 3

Two recent geopolitical events, the Covid pandemic and the war in Ukraine, have had the potential to reduce levels of world trade. To what extent do they appear to have done so? The first, the Covid pandemic, shocked the west when it reduced access to many of the finished and semi-finished products incorporated into supply-chains feeding industrial production. Most critically, micro-chips, used in so many products, ceased to flow, prompting Western – particularly European – producers to start production locally. This process is continuing and will have some impact on the volume of world trade, although this is likely to reduce growth rather than lead to an actual decline in the long term. The same scenario is also likely to play out because of the changes in United States policy in recent years in respect of China and the perceived threat to United States technological and military supremacy posed by large-scale investment in that country.

There are two strands to this policy, one being to pursue a strategic industrial policy to revitalize the United States economy in those areas where it has been perceived to have declined at the expense of China in recent years. The other strand is to ensure that the United States maintains a lasting technological lead over China. This again is unlikely to see a material reduction in world trade; rather, a slowdown in the expected growth as investment from the United States into China is delayed or abandoned.

Jonathan Wakely, a partner at law firm Covington who specialises in national security, says "the approach the administration has taken is to restrict certain categories of investments in what the administration perceives as the most sensitive and problematic technologies."[4]

---

[4] Due Diligence Mergers & Acquisitions. What the US crackdown on Chinese investment actually means. No Attribution. AUGUST 11 2023.
https://www.ft.com/content/cea9630b-b3f7-49ce-8a22-1ddf9c7351bc

We have also noted previously that, with minimal exceptions, countries do not trade with each other. Companies do. Can we assume that this extremely high-volume but limited-in-distribution trade flow is being conducted by a small number of large companies?

Here the World Trade Organization is of little help as it is a grouping of nations, not of the major companies within those nations. It is useful at this point to set out, in its own words, the aims of the WTO:

"At its heart are the WTO agreements, negotiated and signed by the bulk of the world's trading nations. These documents provide the legal ground rules for international commerce. They are essentially contracts, binding governments to keep their trade policies within agreed limits. Although negotiated and signed by governments, the goal is to help producers of goods and services, exporters and importers conduct their business, while allowing governments to meet social and environmental objectives."[5]

From the point of view of countries all this makes sense, in particular the phrase **'while allowing governments to meet social and environmental objectives'**. The role of the company becomes more complex and peripheral because we have already noted that the apparent monolithic multinational company is in fact a web of linked individual companies in a variety of countries. All these countries have governments which should be looking to meet social and environmental goals, although not necessarily all the same ones. For example, a company with a substantial manufacturing facility in Germany may also have a subsidiary with a substantial manufacturing capacity in China. Both employ significant numbers of people, pay taxes, and rely on the facilities of the state (roads, schools, universities, civil order, the rule of law) to function efficiently. Both states should have

---

[5] World Trade Organization website, July 2019.

an interest, on behalf of their citizens, in the legal, social and environmental oversight of the company. The fact that the subsidiary is foreign-owned does not relieve the state from that responsibility, which poses the question of why it has become common belief that power has moved to multinational companies and away from governments. It has not. The truth is that, should they choose to make use of it, all effective power remains with individual governments, subject always to their respective size and political influence.

World Trade Organization

"Competitive struggles among states appear to be producing increasing fragmentation in the regulation of the international economy, in contrast to the comparatively centralized political-economic structures established under American hegemony."[6]

The World Trade Organization (WTO) was the successor organization to the General Agreement on Tariffs and Trade (GATT) set up after the Second World War as part of the creation of a whole raft of multilateral organizations including the United Nations, the International Monetary Fund, and the World Bank. It is important to remember that at this period in history a large part of the world was still controlled by a number of European countries as colonies and that throughout the 1950s and 1960s these colonies slowly gained their independence as sovereign countries but took time to find their feet, both economically and politically, as independent states. The picture was complicated by the ideological war being fought, mainly at an economic level, between the capitalist USA and the communist USSR, and

---

[6] Breaking the WTO, Kristen Hopewell, 2016, Stanford University Press

some of the newly emerging states were being pulled in different directions between these competing ideologies.

The collapse of the USSR at the end of the 1980s changed the dynamic worldwide and coincided with the morphing of the GATT into the WTO. The coming into existence of all these new states underpinned the aim of creating a multilateral basis for them to come together and direct the global trading environment.

"The Westphalian state system that provides the basis for multinational co-operation only expanded globally under US hegemony as mass decolonization following the Second World War resulted in the world being divided into a system of sovereign states."[7]

The move from GATT to the WTO was a profound change, triggered, according to many commentators, by the 'neo-liberal' ideology which overtook large parts of the world in the 1990s. The rules of the GATT were intentionally nonbinding, and states could refuse to comply. "It (GATT) provided room, for example, for states to pursue Keynesian policies directed at maintaining full employment and the post-war welfare state, as well as for developing country governments to intervene in their economies to pursue national development strategies."[8] GATT rules primarily targeted policies "at the border (such as tariffs) and did not interfere significantly with the autonomy of national governments and internal domestic policy making."[9]

The WTO was intended to be something quite different; a permanent organisation with its own dispute-settlement procedures and powerful enforcement mechanisms. To continue the GATT practice of consensus decision-making was a concession which the US was prepared to make as an

---

[7] Breaking the WTO, Kriston Hopewell, 2016, Stanford University Press.
[8] Chorev and Babb, 2009; Ostry 2007.
[9] Ibid.

incentive for countries to agree to the formation of the WTO and because, almost certainly, the US did not doubt its ability to enforce its policies on the new organisation, as it deemed necessary.

At its inception, and for a time after, the WTO appeared to be the multinational organisation which would instil a neutral, overarching governance into the world's trading systems as "the intent of the WTO is to reverse (GATT): to free the 'markets' from politics (both within and between states), by constraining the state and weakening political control over the market."[10]

The proponents of the WTO hoped for continuous and deepening liberalisation of world trade and initially, following the Uruguay Round – the largest ever international trade negotiation, held between 1986 and 1994 under the General Agreement on Tariffs and Trade (GATT) framework and resulting in the creation of the World Trade Organization (WTO) – this aim appeared achievable. It is important to look at whether the project envisioned by the proponents of the WTO is succeeding, or is likely to succeed. If the markets can be 'freed' from politics the role of the state in carving out a new democratic direction for the limited company would be weakened.

Kristen Hopewell supplies compelling argument to show that the WTO as a multilateral, international project has stalled in its intent to continuously extend the liberalisation of international trade. "Brazil and India assumed a more aggressive and activist position in WTO trade negotiations than China and, for much of the Doha Round, which began 2001 but broke down in 2007 following disagreement between the main trading countries and were not resumed, were far more influential in shaping the dynamics and agenda of the negotiations... The rise of Brazil, India and

---

[10] Ibid.

China has destabilized the traditional power structure within the institution, brought an end to the dominance of the US, EU and other advanced-industrialised states..."[11]

We will return to India and China later since India (along with Brazil) is an example of a developing country with a strong and influential corporate lobby capable of influencing government policy. There is every possibility that the onward march of multilateral deregulation stalled in the Doha Round and that, even if it is concluded, its effect will be limited, with no extension of the rules governing international trade.

"Such an outcome is more consistent with the expectations of realism which foresees power struggles, conflict, and a weakening of multilateralism as a result of the emergence of new powers... The rising powers have embraced the core principles supposedly embodied by the WTO: multilateralism, based on the **sovereign equality of states** [my emphasis] engaged in the reciprocal exchange of concessions and free trade. The new world of multipolarity we are entering appears to be one of competing states (and their business actors) engaged in mercantilist struggles."[12]

It is the relationship between those states and the business actors to which this book is directed.

If we accept that the WTO has reached its limit, at least for the foreseeable future, where is the WTO today? The Uruguay Round, as well as reducing tariffs, included agreements on services, investment, and intellectual property. The Agreement on Trade Related Intellectual Property (TRIPS) and the agreement on investment (TRIMS) severely limited the actions countries could take in respect of intellectual property and inward investment; areas where the advanced industrial countries were

---

[11] Kristen Hopewell *Breaking the WTO*
[12] Ibid.

dominant. Further expansion of WTO rules in these areas is now limited, if not blocked, so that emphasis has switched to the rapidly expanding area of bilateral and regional free-trade agreements.

Amongst economists there is increasing interest in free trade agreements. In a thought-provoking paper Danni Rodrik suggests, "Rather than reining in protectionists, trade agreements empower another set of special interests and politically well-connected firms, such as international banks, pharmaceutical companies, and multinational corporations. Such agreements may result in freer, mutually beneficial trade, through exchange of market access. But they are as likely to produce welfare-reducing, or purely redistributive outcomes under the guise of free trade."[13]

This change came about largely in the movement from GATT to the WTO as free trade agreements moved away from being largely concerned with import tariffs and quotas to increasingly focus on domestic rules and regulations. The economist's standard unit in respect of such agreements is the 'nation'. Trade agreements are between nations and to the benefit of those nations. However, trade agreements are not initiated by citizens but almost exclusively by companies or by trade associations. Such agreements only benefit the nation, in the true sense, if its internal arrangements pass those benefits (increased trade volumes and increased profits for companies) on to the citizen.

In respect of cross-border capital movements, Rodrik rightly notes that these clauses became popular as many economists and the International Monetary Fund began to question free capital flows, especially in times of economic crisis.

I was in Asia in 1998, at the time of the Asian Financial

---

[13] Danni Rodrik, Journal of Economic Perspectives - Volume 32, number 2 - Spring 2018 Pages 73 -90.

Crisis, on an Asia-Pacific board with subsidiary companies in almost every Asian country. It was interesting to note that the only country which escaped major economic collapse at that time was Malaysia, which imposed capital controls, to great international outcry.

Probably the most controversial clauses in trade agreements and those most actively sought by companies are investor-state dispute settlement clauses. Originally intended to be included in the agreements between developed and 'under-developed' countries where the rule of law may have been less certain, they have expanded to become ubiquitous. Rodrik believes this is difficult to justify "among advanced countries with well-functioning legal systems". I would go further and judge such clauses to be unacceptable.

Rodrik mentions the then proposed Transatlantic Trade and Investment Partnership between the United States and the European Union. My view is clearly shared by a substantial body of opinion in the European Union as this agreement was rejected, predominantly because of such an investor protection clause. This took place because the European Union, uniquely, is transparent in its negotiations with third countries and its citizens were able to see what was being proposed.

The European Union is also – if not unique – notable for its desire to harmonise regulatory standards at a technical level where it can aid trade and, as far as social standards are concerned, to standardise them at a high level. At this level, regulatory harmonisation is reasonable. What is not acceptable is "investors, banks, and multinational companies seeking to increase rents at the expense of the general interest... these are fundamentally trade deals. They are not negotiations on public health, regulatory experimentation, promoting structural change and industrialization in developing nations, or protecting labor standards in the advanced economies."[14]

My own interest in this subject, and the inception of this book, occurred at the time I was living in the Far East. Shortly after the Asian Financial Crisis, the German newspaper Die Zeit included a series of what were for me influential and thought-provoking articles on 'turbo-capitalism'.

Turbo-capitalism uses the assets we all need as humans in the modern world: water, power, raw materials, social services, commodities and even food, as chips in a game of chance in a financial casino which has few players, the majority of whom are uninterested in any damage their actions may cause to the citizen.

It is a result of the financialization of productive assets, both private and public, and socially necessary: the financial structure of a company with high levels of leverage (borrowing), speculation in derivatives and other financial instruments to extract value and pay dividends becomes more important than the financial health, stability, and often the very existence of, the company.

One of the full-page articles was an interview with Edward Luttwak, an economist with the Center for Strategic and International Studies in Washington, who had just published his book, Turbo-Kapitalismus.

Die Zeit put the question to Luttwak as to how a country could defend itself against turbo-capitalism. His answer is worth noting, only then, when the phenomenon has been correctly analysed and a central question has been answered: "should society serve the economy, or should the economy serve society? In America and England [sic] it is self-evident that society must adjust – like a piece of putty."[15]

---

[14] The Globalization Paradox, Dani Rodrik, Oxford University Press, 2011.
[15] Turbo-Kapitalismus, Edward Luttwak, 1999, Europa Verlag, Hamburg.

Luttwak triggered the first clue, that the solution lies at the level of the nation state, and no further.

On the same date, Die Welt published an article by Edzard Reuter (who died in October 2024 aged ninety-six); a respected, senior German businessman who had been the Chairman of the Management Board of Daimler-Benz until 1995. Quoting Guenter Grass, who had attacked uncontrolled capitalism as a risk to society, Reuter asked a profound question: is it the case that businesspeople are the drivers of this activity, or are they the driven?

The impression that most businesspeople are the driven seems apt. They appear to be prisoners of a dogma originating in the USA, echoed in support by the City of London and in all the finance centres of the world.

At the same time, the worldwide active businesses change their character. They begin to change their multinational character – in the sense of a well-organised interaction of relatively independent businesses which understand themselves to be "good corporate citizens" in an essentially national arena – into transnational entities which bit by bit loose themselves from their original location.

When one considers the speed and dimensions of such activity, the question must be raised as to whether a material part of the finance markets – and with them the whole economy – is not a part of what a scientist would call a closed system, which follows its own laws and whose course is scarcely capable of being influenced externally. It therefore runs into the danger of accelerating independently like an avalanche, and perhaps this avalanche threatens to wipe away the primacy of politics.

Involved in this possible system are three groups of actors: the institutional investors, the banks, and the managements of internationally active businesses.

It is worth quoting fully a paragraph from Reuter's article and then drawing conclusions from it.

"A true sense of responsibility remains directed at more than only the material interests of the provider of funds. It includes the people who are dependent on the business. And it aims to benefit society in which the business operates. Only someone who has understood this can contribute to keeping alive the ethic which alone is capable of legitimating business activity. The framework for these responsibilities remains the function of the state. That does not change the conclusion that none of us knows the answer how this challenge in respect of the drivers of globalization can be solved."[16]

The views of Reuter raised two thoughts: firstly that if such a respected businessman was disturbed by turbo-capitalism and believed many of his contemporaries were driven and not the drivers, this was probably true. Secondly that the solution lay at the level of the nation state and that if many senior managers were either driving actively in a closed system or were being driven in that same system, then the sooner the steering wheel was either removed from their grasp or at the very least made more difficult to operate, the better. Equally, the belief that all senior management would reject a tightening of their field of operation is unlikely to be true.

Edzard Reuter's fears were by no means unprecedented; they had been preceded and echoed by many well-known world figures.

In the decades following Reuter's article, a number of thoughtful academic books have been written to explore and seek solutions to this challenge. In The Corporation, Joel Bakan clearly identifies the problem and in The Silent Takeover Noreena Hertz analyses and describes the effect of global capitalism and its challenge to democracy. Her new agenda includes the need for the 'disenfranchisement' of corporations and crucially the checking of the power of

---

[16] Edzard Reuter, Article Die Welt, 9th December 1999

corporations at a national level but does not detail how this should be done.

In 2011, Danni Rodrik published The Globalisation Paradox, a masterly exposition of the then current state of play in respect of globalisation. Rodrik's belief is summarised in his foreword: "Democracies have the right to protect their social arrangements and when this right clashes with the requirements of the global economy it is the latter that should give way."

Whilst all academic writers are agreed that much of the problem lies with the role of the company and international groups of companies, most still see the problem as a global one, the solution to which should or must include global bodies or organisations and where necessary their reform.

This leads me to conclude that perhaps part of the problem in seeking a way forward is because of the widespread use of the word 'globalisation'.

Rodrik's subtext is that global markets, states and democracy cannot co-exist. I believe this is too widely drawn. Markets have always existed, and for long periods have been global. It is necessary to dig deeper and to propose that limited liability companies in their transnational form, including the three actors mentioned previously (institutional investors, banks[17], and the managements of internationally active businesses), operating as part of a closed system, cannot in their present form co-exist with states and democracy.

The emphasis on globalisation gives the impression that we are dealing with a new phenomenon, the cure for which must

---

[17] It is essential to remember that banks also operate through the medium of the limited company and are therefore capable of being dealt with in the same way as the non-banking company. Since they operate in a defined sector of the economy, the action necessary here may differ from that needed in the case of a non-banking company.

be global, as the symptoms clearly are. This may well be incorrect and the challenges facing the economies of the mature states may be better analysed by naming much of what we have experienced over the last forty years not as globalisation but as **turbo-capitalism**. This overall term better reflects the activities which give rise to the type of challenges we have been dealing with for a long time, but over which nation states have chosen to relinquish control.

We want to know why nation states have chosen to take this step, to confirm that it is not inevitable, and to outline a detailed programme of legislation for taking back control. It is not possible to do so for the whole world so the detailed programme put forward in this book will be focused on the United Kingdom.

The most pressing reason for focusing on the UK is that this country has the weakest and most antiquated company law, and the greatest propensity amongst the Western democracies (after the USA) to pander to corporate demands.

Of current interest is the fact that the UK has left the European Union so its legal system will no longer be directly influenced by EU legislation. Changes to company law can be made unilaterally and the legal system can be considered in isolation.

More worrying is the historic experience of the United Kingdom in weakening rather than strengthening its company law; a trend that must be reversed.

Chapter 2
British Globalisation v Turbo-capitalism

"Private capital tends to become concentrated in few hands,
partly because of competition among the capitalists, and
partly because technological development and the increasing
division of labor encourage the formation of larger units of
production at the expense of smaller ones. The result of these
developments is an oligarchy of private capital the enormous
power of which cannot be effectively checked even by a
democratically organised political society."

Why Socialism? Albert Einstein, May 1949

Einstein goes on to explain that political parties are largely
financed by private capital and that it is their interests
which are served, to the exclusion of the citizen and
underprivileged parts of society.

Since private capital also controls, directly or indirectly,
the media it is difficult for the citizen to gain a true picture
and make informed political decisions.

Terms such as 'social values', 'social principles' and 'social
goals' need to return to political discourse. When the much-
misunderstood term 'globalisation' is discussed and debated,
the recurring myth is propagated that this must result in a
levelling down of national social, environmental and,
sometimes, human rights, as otherwise companies will move
to where the lowest standards prevail, with the resulting
loss of jobs, a fall in GDP, and the inevitable societal
insecurity and uncertainty.

This is not true. Some companies would undoubtedly do
this, but for most it simply is not possible. In arguing that
the nation state, in this case Britain, has to regain control
over the limited company, it has to be made clear that

governments have bought in to the arguments put forward by vested interests not because of fear of consequences but because this is an ideology they support and believe in. The myths of 'globalisation' are a useful cloak behind which to hide unpopular political choices.

The examples given below are all perfectly legal, both in respect of UK company and tax law, and such situations are not uncommon.

Petrochemicals, A Reduction in Skilled Employment and Productivity

In 2025, Scotland's only oil refinery stopped processing crude oil at Grangemouth as it transitioned to becoming an import terminal for finished fuels. This will have the effect of increasing the British trade deficit as a result of importing more expensive product and reducing productivity, with fewer skilled jobs and less investment. Refining operations are instead being expanded at Lavera in France.
This situation, multiplied on a national scale, is part of the explanation for falling British productivity.
"Ineos has told workers {2013} it will close its Grangemouth petrochemicals plant after they refused to sign up to a cost-cutting plan deemed vital for its survival... Ineos said it will appoint liquidators to the business within a week." It was also "warned that the closure of the petrochemical unit could be followed by a shutdown of the adjacent refinery, operated in partnership with Petro-China [a subsidiary of the Chinese state oil company], which provides 80% of Scotland's fuel."[18]
As an individual case this is interesting as the Chinese had

---

[18] Daily Telegraph October 23rd 2013

paid US$1 billion in 2011 for a stake in the joint ventures, including Grangemouth, with Ineos. Two years later, they are apparently agreeing to close a major part of them.

Quoting from the European Union approval for the creation of the joint ventures: "The envisaged transaction relates to the creation of three ventures {JVs} jointly controlled by Ineos and PetroChina as part of a single transaction. The JVs will include the refining assets at Grangemouth (Scotland) and Lavera (France) and related businesses, all currently wholly owned by Ineos."[19]

What the European Union was confirming with this decision was that despite PetroChina controlling one part the business and Ineos another, they judged that both companies had joint control over the whole business.

So, the Chinese state oil company and Ineos threaten to close a key UK asset with resulting liquidation. Why would we consider this surprising? Because only eight years previously, in 2005, Ineos had bought the assets from BP.

What Ineos needed, however, was money – a cool $9bn. Three banks – Barclays Capital, Merrill Lynch and Morgan Stanley – agreed to stump up the cash for the acquisition.

"Ineos had taken on a lot of debt to fund the BP deal. The downturn halved its earnings. The company cut capital expenditure, maintenance, salaries and bonuses. The banks moved in, extracting €804m in fees. Ineos eventually convinced the banks it should stay in charge."[20]

[19] REGULATION (EC) No 139/2004 MERGER PROCEDURE Case No COMP/M.6151 - PETROCHINA/ INEOS/ JV
Notification of 5.04.2011 pursuant to Article 4 of Council Regulation No 139/20041
Publication in the Official Journal of the European Union No C 116, 14.04.2011, p.11
[20] Ineos Group Ltd. Jim Ratcliffe The reticent billionaire is one of the most successful of British entrepreneurs but also one of the most controversial Sylvia Pfeifer November 20 2014. https://www.ft.com/content/9318986c-8ec2-11e3-b6f1-00144feab7de 0

The reason given in 2013 for closure was that the business was loss-making and without cost-cutting (cutting wages and benefits) the plant was not viable.

The BBC tried to gain an insight into these claims and into the financial position of the companies concerned. It proved difficult: "I've been given a bit more insight into its financial operations, following the Unite claims that things aren't as bad as they're being painted. I got confirmation that the £579m four-year 'loss' claim is not a loss in conventional terms."[21]

The BBC noted that of the £579 million, £110 million was trading loss and the rest mostly capital expenditure, also noting that companies usually only invested if they expected future profits. They also observed that the site was operated by a number of companies, including one based in Switzerland, the complex structure making it almost impossible for an outsider to analyse the financial statements.

It is traditional to think that 'globalisation' presents the risk to working conditions, tax income to the state, and the role and security of major economic entities within a state or region, but this is too simplistic.

The threat is equally present, from what Edzard Reuter so clearly spelled out in 1999, those three groups of actors: the institutional investors, the banks, and the management of internationally active businesses.

As to his question about whether these actors are the drivers or the driven, in the case of Grangemouth they are clearly the drivers.

This is turbo-capitalism.

---

[21] 18 October 2013 Shedding light on Grangemouth Douglas Fraser, BBC Business and economy editor, Scotland.
https://www.bbc.co.uk/news/uk-scotland-scotland-business-24580313

And how is it steered and enabled? Through a labyrinth of limited liability companies, all legally independent but operating where it is beneficial as an integrated unit.

It is both pointless and to an extent unfair to direct criticism at the actors involved in these operations; businesspeople will always seize available opportunities at the least cost and with the minimum overview and control.

Only the state and its control over company law can lay down the legal basis to enable businesses to incorporate but with the proviso that the law protects not only shareholders (owners) but also the citizen, and the state itself.

In 2025 the Prax Group also collapsed into compulsory liquidation; a group which includes the Lindsey oil refinery, which supplies around 10% of the UK's fuel. Newspaper reports indicated that the group owed the UK tax authorities in the region of £250 million.[22] As always, the British Government expressed anger and outrage but nevertheless took no steps to introduce any law that would prevent these constant failures. It can only be assumed that they encourage failure.

Any hope that a British government of any political colour will change direction is useless, as reported by the Financial Times (UK infrastructure financing on track to reach record high, 8th September 2025):

"Around $38bn of debt was issued in the first eight months of this year on 90 mergers and acquisitions, refinancing and other deals, according to data from Infralogic. That rate of monthly issuance puts the UK on a path to raise at least $57bn in infrastructure borrowing by the end of the year. Alexander MacLeod, head of data analysis at Infralogic, said the number of deals showed that the 'UK infrastructure market is robust and even the troubles at Thames haven't

---

[22] Financial Times, 4.7.2025

shaken the appetite for the essential regulated utilities...'

"'The UK government has also shown its commitment to private finance, which will have reassured investors.'

"Global financial players are drawn to the UK by stable, government-backed income from British households for essential infrastructure — such as waste, energy, water and telecoms services — and by generous state support, which can protect investments against large losses or risks."[23]

Risks to the Elderly

Southern Cross Group

A different problem arises when private companies take over the operating of socially necessary care facilities, which are largely funded by the state. Here, turbo-capitalism can inflict considerable damage on vulnerable people, both directly and through the fear of a service not being available. A classic example of this in operation was the rapid growth and subsequent failure of the Southern Cross Group. Here again, employment insecurity and extremely low pay are not a result of 'globalisation' but of the controllable excesses of turbo-capitalism.

Until the financial excesses of the 1990s and early 2000s, most care homes were small scale businesses, and often family-run.

As any income-producing asset can be used as a financial tool, there was no reason the homes caring for elderly people could not be harnessed to this end. An overview of the growth and downfall of the group reveals the classic pattern of rapid growth funded by borrowing, made worse in this

---

[23] Financial Times (UK infrastructure financing on track to reach record high, 8th September 2025)

case using sale and leaseback of the company's properties both to fund future growth and to provide another saleable unit. At the time of the Southern Cross Group's collapse, 31,000 elderly people lived in its homes; around ten per cent of the UK's elderly care home population.

In overview, the story is not untypical; by 2002, Southern Healthcare was a significant operator, with 140 sites. Venture capital firm West LB bought the company for £80 million as part of a management buyout. Two years later, US private equity firm Blackstone acquired the company and went on to buy NHP, one of Southern Cross's largest landlords, in a £1.1 billion deal which increased the companies' size by another 192 homes.

Following further acquisitions, NHP was sold in 2006, followed by the flotation of Southern Cross on the stock market that summer. Blackstone finally exited in 2007. In 2008, the financial crash began the group's demise. There were a number of reasons for the collapse: high borrowing levels, onerous lease terms with high annual increases which had enabled the property-owning company to be sold at a premium, and even cutbacks by local authorities in their level of payments for residents.

No state or its citizens should allow a situation to develop where vulnerable elderly people are put in such a situation.

There was much handwringing at the time, with proposals for better regulation of the care for the elderly, but the most obvious solution was ignored.

Where the state supports vulnerable people in any context, and pays private companies to look after them, a special class of company is required, with higher minimum capital requirements and where the directors have specific responsibilities to ensure that the company is able to meet its obligations in the medium term, with a clear obligation to trigger early warnings of financial or other problems.

It is always wise to dig beneath the surface of failed public companies, since we have already seen that they are simply a grouping of often smaller individual companies with their own boards of directors operating a specific unit; in this case, one or more homes for the elderly.

In the case of Southern Cross, one such subsidiary was Ashbourne Life Limited. In an earlier era, this would have been a small, sound company, profitable for modest investors. In 2008, it had a turnover of £10.2 million and a profit of £555,000. What was different in this context is that in 2007 the company had net assets and retained earnings of £2.6 million but in 2008 these, together with that year's profits, were paid out by a £3 million dividend to the parent company. Following this, the company, with a share capital of £1, had retained earnings of £193,000. At least a positive figure. Note 16 to the financial statements tells us that the company had "provided cross-guarantees (each company promising to pay the debts, if necessary, of the other) in relation to bank and other borrowings of other group undertakings amounting to £87.5 million".

Ashbourne Life Limited's funds were held in the bank account of Southern Cross Healthcare Limited. The company appeared to have four directors, although a number of directors appeared and disappeared at regular intervals.

What were these directors doing? It can be assumed that they were managing the day-to-day business, but in any event the company went into Company Voluntary Agreement in 2010, along with the rest of the group. The old, damaging legal fiction is that whilst a holding company has complete control over a subsidiary and, apparently, over its directors, the two are completely separate legal entities and the holding company can walk away at any time. This has to be challenged.

Risks to Public Provision of Services

Carillion

The collapse of Carillion PLC caused shockwaves in government and industry because of the number of outsourced government contracts the group held. This collapse culminated in the group's auditors, KPMG, settling a £1.3 billion lawsuit brought by Carillion's liquidators. The collapse of the company with £7 billion of debt resulted in 3000 job losses "and caused chaos across hundreds of its projects and public sector works, including schools, roads, prisons, and even Liverpool FC's stadium, Anfield. It also delayed the construction of two new hospitals: the 646-bed Royal Liverpool and 669-bed Midland Metropolitan in Sandwell, West Midlands, which were due to open in 2017 and 2018 respectively, resulting in the projects running hundreds of millions of pounds over budget."[24]

The effect of such collapses is felt also by pensioners and potential pensioners of the group.

The Pension Regulator reported: "We immediately opened an investigation to establish the circumstances that had led to the insolvency and the impact on the pension savers... There were around 350 entities within the Group structure, 19 of which were participating employers to 13 defined benefit pension schemes, which had a combined estimated deficit on a buy-out basis of circa £1.8 billion at the end of 2016... In the circumstances, there was no prospect of

---

[24] KPMG settles £1.3bn lawsuit from Carillion creditors over alleged negligence. Collapse of outsourcer in 2018 with debts of £7bn came after annual accounts were approved by KPMG. Kalyeena Makortoff
@kalyeena Fri 17 Feb 2023 18.25 GMT
https://www.theguardian.com/business/2023/feb/17/kpmg-pays-13bn-to-settle-negligent-auditing-claim-by-carillion-creditors

securing a Contribution Notice based on the evidence of Carillion PLC's public misstatement of its financial performance {that is, no money to get back}. The Carillion Group's insolvency has had a significant impact on its pension schemes, and the benefits savers will receive."[25]

This leads at once to the proposition that primary regulation is preferable to secondary monitoring. However well conducted, secondary monitoring is rarely effective and is much more expensive than primary monitoring.

Interserve

A second major outsourcing company, Interserve, has now gone into administration, with a debt load of £815 million and here, as always, it is informative to go below the surface of the group and look at some of the individual businesses.

The West Yorkshire Community Rehabilitation Company Limited warrants investigation. From the financial statement for the year ended December 31st 2017, the following information can be extracted (bearing in mind that this is less than two years before the collapse of the group in which this company was a subsidiary):

"The company's principal activity during the period is the provision of community rehabilitation services. Under the umbrella of Transforming Rehabilitation, we deliver the sentence of the court (probation) through accredited programmes, community payback and unpaid work. In addition, we provide rehabilitation services that reduce re-offending."

Financially, the company is, to use an understatement, not

[25] The Pensions Regulator. The Carillion Group, Regulatory intervention report. https://www.thepensionsregulator.gov.uk/en/document-library/enforcement-activity/regulatory-intervention-reports/carillion-group-regulatory-intervention-report

doing very well: "The reoffending data is not as expected at bid stage which has had a detrimental impact on profit... To this end an onerous contract provision of £5.7 million has been made in the 2017 accounts."

In fact, the company is doing so badly that the auditors would have difficulty giving an unqualified audit opinion, which is that the company can survive another year, without a support guarantee from the ultimate holding company. What form this support 'guarantee' was in, and how enforceable in law, would be known only to the directors and auditors.

"In the event that operating cash flows would not cover all the company's financial obligations then the company has received confirmation from its ultimate parent company, that sufficient financial support will be provided to enable the company to meet its obligations as they fall due. The directors have further satisfied themselves that the ultimate parent company has sufficient financial resources to provide such support if called upon... And as a result, they continue to adopt the going concern basis in preparing the annual report and financial statements."

In 2016, the company made a loss of £1 million on a turnover of £17.9 million and in 2017 a loss of £6.6 million on a turnover of £16.0 million, after providing £5.8 million for onerous contracts. Interesting, you may say. Even more interesting is that the company had a share capital of £11,000. that is not a misprint: £11,000, with £10,000 contributed by the shareholders and £1,000 in preference shares by the government. The preference shares held by the government carry the following information:

"This type of share is only issued to, held by and transferred to the crown (the Government) and does not carry an entitlement to share in the capital or profits of the company."

This is typical of the 19th century arcane thinking about

company law and the management of limited companies. We will look later at the need for a special type of company where the state and state activities and funding are concerned, but the reader may well ask why, for such critical services, the directors are not legally obliged to maintain a minimum and adequate level of capital in this company, to address the obvious insecurities in the funding and contractual relations of the company (the directors were also directors of a number of other similar companies).

Under British company law, directors have only a responsibility to their shareholders, and this also applies to a private limited company set up to perform critical and sensitive work involving offenders and ex-offenders out in the community. Having seen the reality behind the glossy public relations annual statements of major public companies involved in outsourcing government activity, the reader may well be dismayed.

The change in the structure of the United Kingdom's economy has been a constant cause of comment. Reviewing a book on Britain's industrial decline in 2013, Robert Skidelsky, a respected economic historian and author and founder of the Social Market Foundation, noted:

"In the early 1950s, Britain was an industrial giant. Today, it is an industrial pygmy. Manufacturing was industry's bedrock. In 1952, it produced a third of the national output, employed 40 per cent of the workforce and made up a quarter of world manufacturing exports. Today, manufacturing in this country accounts for just 9.8 (today 8.8% per cent of GDP, employs only 8 (today 7%) per cent of the workforce and sells 2 per cent of the world's manufacturing exports."[26]

Skidelsky suggested two prime causes for this decline: the

---

[26] New Statesman January 24th 2013. Review of Meeting our Makers, Britain's Long Industrial Decline, the slow death of British Industry, a 60 year suicide 1952-2012.

imperial legacy, and erratic government policy.

Until the 1960s, much of the United Kingdom's trade was with the empire or its remnants and maintaining the sterling area meant high interest rates and an overvalued exchange rate detrimental to manufacturing. Although erratic government policy certainly played a role in decline, equal weight should be given to the role of the City of London, one of the world's leading financial centres at the heart of an economically declining country. This role had already been identified.

Skidelsky quotes Michael Heseltine, when president of the Board of Trade in 1993, before Parliament: "They have encouraged growth in companies by acquisition and financial engineering rather than organic development and building up products and markets. They have led us to place far too great an emphasis on comparisons of near-term financial results in judging our companies instead of considering the strength of management and its underlying strategy."

Although this observation and criticism dates back to 1993, the same attitude continued and is still prevalent today.

To show the dangers of financialization in respect to major and often strategically key companies and services, it will be necessary to look at recent history. Influential was Harold Geneen, an American businessman active in the 1960s and 1970s who was responsible for transforming ITT (the International Telephone and Telegraph Company), where he became chief executive in 1961, into a huge multinational conglomerate. ITT's results improved rapidly, which increased its share price and price/earnings ratio, enabling Geneen to acquire other companies using ITT stock. At the end of a sixteen-year period, ITT owned 350 companies in eighty different countries. The management practices promoted by Geneen were set out in his book Managing and were eagerly adopted by business schools, management gurus and other businesspeople. He can be credited with – if not inventing – at least accelerating what became known as 'management by objectives'. All this preceded the financial collapse of ITT, which shrank rapidly.

To Geneen, trained as an accountant, management was simple. All one had to do was decide what profit increase was needed each year, say 10%, and use the financial figures to reach the financial objective. Sales must be increased, and costs slashed, in each department and by every individual, this to be achieved by incentives for success in meeting targets and punishment for failure, which could often mean dismissal. That this ignorant nonsense could dominate Western management thinking for decades is scarcely credible, but true.

Sadly, one of the few areas where this mentality is still common is in government, where ministers still call for a '10% improvement in efficiency' in one public service or another without any idea what this might involve or without providing the funding to enable this to take place.

Younger readers will need reminding of British manufacturing icons, Imperial Chemical Industries (ICI) and General Electric (GE). The website This is Money reported in 2007 that the nation had watched one of its greatest blue-chip industrial companies (ICI) sold off along with Corus (the old British Steel), the British Oxygen Company (BOC) and Glassmaker Pilkington. Other such companies included British Plaster Board and the shipping and ports giant P+O. These sell-offs meant enormous consequences for the country's economy and tax base. With the departure overseas of companies like P+O "go the headquarters, thousands of staff, the nation's research and development capability, and a chunk of the nation's corporate tax base."[27]

The government of the day was given assurances that ICI's

---

[27] Ibid.

research and development would remain in the UK. Two years later it was transferred abroad.

The events at General Electric, which became Marconi, are even more disturbing. General Electric was a well-managed group, with profits of £1 billion a year and with a cash reserve of £3 billion. However, the 'City' (the City of London, Britain's financial centre) was not satisfied, and 'investors' complained that growth was too slow. To assist him, the managing director employed a former S.G. Warburg investment banker, already well known for his part in breaking up ICI. The power arm and the defence business were floated in France or sold off. This raised an astonishing £8 billion to add to the £3 billion cash reserve. In four years of deal-making, during which the City earned substantial sums, the management burned through both the £3 billion and the £8 billion, and left the company with £3 billion of debt. In a debt-for-equity swap (turning loans into share capital), shareholders retained 0.5% of the new company, Marconi Corporation plc. In October 2005, the Swedish firm Ericsson offered to buy the Marconi name and most of the assets.

Both ICI and GE are examples of how the UK's industrial base was destroyed despite, or possibly because of, the country having a world-leading financial centre. Further evidence that secondary monitoring has largely failed. Whether this failure is deliberate policy or incompetence, the regularity of failure and its continuation must lead to the conclusion that it is policy; one would like to assume that no government could be so incompetent.

The general decline in UK industrial production and with it the loss of jobs and levels of income was to some extent blamed on globalisation in the 1980s and onwards but came from a different direction. The level of offshoring of industrial production during this period owed more to the sale of large sections of UK industry to foreign competitors, and their later dismemberment.

Another cause of the breakdown in the social contract was internal (home) outsourcing, where layers of companies and agencies provided ever cheaper services with ever worsening employment conditions.

Finally, reduced capital investment and the resulting fall in overall productivity led to an inevitable worsening of employment conditions as companies cut expenditure in the only way they knew: by reducing labour costs.

None of the above analysis is the result of 'globalisation'; it is simply home-grown turbo-capitalism.

Chapter 3
Holding Companies

A holding company is simply the organisation at the top of a chain of multi-layered company ownership which can cover many countries and continents. Should you feel up to reading the financial statements of BP – with twenty-three pages of in total probably over one thousand related companies – bear this complexity in mind.

This is the result of the most far-reaching, yet at the time the least remarked on, extension of company law which occurred in the 1860s. There was no new law; the Court of Appeal in two landmark cases, Barned's and Asiatic Banking (both related to banking and finance), found corporate membership – that is, one company owning another company – to be compatible with the Companies Act 1862 (Mackie)[28] and the courts reached "their conclusion that inter-company stock ownership was contemplated, or at least not forbidden, under the statuary scheme".[29] All this thirty years before the landmark 1897 legal case of Salomon, and Salomon and Co Ltd, which anchored the separation of the company as a legal entity from its owner(s).

This development was neither inevitable nor necessarily beneficial but resulted from a rapid deregulation of company law leading to a banking crisis in the mid-1860s, during which banks and finance companies tried to disclaim liabilities associated with shareholdings by arguing that their ownership was unlawful. The cases which gave rise to these decisions were exactly the opposite of what you would

---

[28] Lecturer in Law, School of Law, University of Aberdeen. Article was presented at a seminar held at the Centre for Corporate and Commercial Law (3CL) at the University of Cambridge on the 27 October 2015.

[29] Limited Liability and Corporate Groups, Phillip Blumberg (1986).

expect, in that companies argued that they were not legally allowed to own other companies, and the court – to protect the financial health of the country – decided that they could. There was no great moral or philosophical debate on this major legal step, so there can be no need to reflect too deeply on amending this aspect of the law.

The long-term, unintended consequences of these legal decisions, made under intense pressure and where any wider consequences were not considered, can be seen today. The idea that British company law developed in a structured, thoughtful manner after careful consideration of its long-term effect on society and its overall purpose in relation to the state and the citizen is so far from the truth that it is scarcely worth pursuing. What must be pursued, however, is the effect which the tier upon tier of limited liability companies within international groups can have on the state and its citizens.

The automatic assumption that limited liability, with the separate legal existence of an unlimited number of companies owned by other companies in multiple levels of ownership, is the norm, has become axiomatic. Professor Blumberg, with others, questions the legitimacy of this assumption: "The extension of layers of limited liability to the tiers of subsidiaries within corporate groups lacks most of the theoretical justification that has been advanced in defence of the rule."[30]

This is an early example of the role the courts have played, and continue to play, in defining and extending company law.

---

[30] Limited Liability and Corporate Groups, Phillip Blumberg (1986).

Multi-national Groups
with a British Holding Company

In the case of a single company or a holding company with only United Kingdom subsidiaries, it is possible to legislate to remove limited liability from subsidiaries. What is the situation where a United Kingdom holding company has an overseas subsidiary?

Whilst the foreign subsidiary is controlled by the United Kingdom holding company, it is subject to the legal requirements of the host country in all respects as to capital structure and maintenance, management, and the levying of corporate taxes. This is as you would expect. Although large multinational companies appear monolithic when reviewed through the prism of detailed and colourful consolidated financial statements, the underlying detail is extremely messy, with local managements following local legal, taxation, employment, environmental, and criminal laws whilst still trying to follow guidelines and rules set out by the parent company. This effectively means that the local subsidiary keeps two sets of financial statements: one for local purposes and one for consolidation with those of the holding company. Clearly the ones that count are the local records, as they decide in real terms how profitable the company is. Tax paid is tax paid.

Looking at the consolidated financial statements of major international companies, it is too easy to forget how a large subsidiary in any country must be managed. Multiplied by tens or hundreds of such companies, a huge challenge is created for head office management, and for auditors.

I have experience in this area, if somewhat dated. Early in my career, I was an auditor with a top four audit firm. In the mid-1970s I audited a major European construction material company with a large subsidiary in Italy. After the completion of the formal audit, we were somewhat surprised to be told that we would now be given access to the 'B' books. Three of us were driven into the hills outside the city to a farmhouse, where we were presented with ledgers and bearer bank books containing transactions not disclosed to the tax authorities. The local management had to do this as, being a subsidiary of another company, non-disclosure could have been construed as fraud.

Another example (one of many) occurred in Brazil in the early 1980s as my career in audit was ending. The Brazilian subsidiary of a large European engineering company was audited and in the closing meeting the very capable financial head was asked whether all the tax affairs were up to date and if there were any outstanding issues with the tax authorities. He explained that no, there were no issues. Every year, two tax inspectors would arrive to check the records. They arrived by train and in the evening left through the goods outwards department where, hanging on a hook, were the keys to two new cars which the inspectors drove home. There were never any queries.

I make no comment on the outcome of these disclosures; they are in the distant past. Today, auditors are constantly faced with similar dilemmas and must meet the legal and ethical requirements of the countries in which they audit, and of international standards.

As the British Government has secured the capitalisation and management of British companies, what is its responsibility in respect of overseas subsidiaries? The short answer is none; this must be the sole responsibility of the host country. If that country chooses a lax system of company law and taxation, that government must answer to its own citizens. What responsibility does the United Kingdom Government have to protect the assets of the overseas subsidiary company of a United Kingdom holding company? I would argue that, again, it has none.

International business is a risk and, before engaging in a business venture abroad, due diligence is needed. Where risk is perceived as high, it should be avoided. No company is forced to do business; it is an informed choice, with the possibility of profit or loss, and must remain the responsibility of the individual company. Clearly each country will wish to secure the safety of its citizens and will expect every other country to ensure their safety.

Following the logic of viewing a limited liability company as a legal fiction, a name on a piece of paper, the company's safety cannot be in danger. It would be reasonable to expect that, in the case of expropriation, the expropriating country would pay a market restitution, but in today's world we would not expect a war to break out if this was not the case.

These arguments apply equally in the case of an overseas holding company with a subsidiary in the United Kingdom. There could be no accusations of discrimination as all rules and regulations would apply equally to all companies.

This is not the view that large multi-national companies have persuaded many governments to adopt: that it is their responsibility to remove risk from the business activities of companies worldwide, even at the cost of severely limiting those governments room for action, often in respect of working and environmental standards relating to their own citizens.

Chapter 4
Banks and Finance Companies

British journalist Mick Davis first coined the phrase in 1984 that the UK is 'a financial capital with a medium-sized country attached', so before considering the future of the limited liability company in general we should first consider it in the specific context of banking and finance.

The Companies Act 2006 has little to say about banks. Section 1164 of the 2006 Act defines a banking company and a banking group in the context of the Financial Services and Marketing Act 2000. A bank incorporated as a private limited company or a public limited company is subject to all the requirements of the Companies Act 2006, including the requirements on directors, but these are limited. This is a complex area and can only be touched on, but it is important in the interest of completeness and in view of the size of the financial sector in relation to the whole UK economy. The International Monetary Fund produced a country report No 22/57 on the United Kingdom in February 2022 and the first line of the opening paragraph states: "the UK financial sector is globally systemic, open, and complex".

Banking and finance companies are regulated in the UK by three bodies: the Bank of England (BoE), the Prudential Regulation Authority (PRA), and the Financial Conduct Authority (FCA), under the legislative framework of the Financial Services and Markets Act 2000. The regulatory framework has also been influenced by European Union laws which set minimum requirements for the regulation of banks and banking services for the European Economic Area. After Brexit, the European Union (Withdrawal) Act 2018 incorporated EU legislation and regulation into United Kingdom domestic law; to be discussed is how far the UK intends to deviate from these rules in the future and the likely effect of such deviation.

The PRA and the FCA are the lead regulators for banks, whilst the BoE is the resolution authority responsible for regulatory intervention and for banks failing or likely to fail. The PRA is the prudential regulator and the FCA the conduct regulator for banks. The BoE and the PRA monitor about 1500 banks and insurance companies, not all resident in the UK, and from the BoE list of banks from October 3rd 2022 (taken in conjunction with the list of approximately 400 limited company credit unions monitored by the BoE as of July 1st 2022), it can reasonably be estimated that about a half of the 1500 monitored bodies are UK resident, and the majority are limited companies. The rest are branches of non-resident insurance companies, banks incorporated outside of the United Kingdom but authorised to accept deposits through a branch in the United Kingdom, or banks incorporated in the European Economic Area.

The PRA is also responsible for monitoring the 'ring fencing' of retail and proprietary banking activity within large banks.

From the PRA Annual Report for 2022 we learn: "Ring fencing has been in effect since 1st January 2019. It requires UK banking groups with more than £25 billion of core deposits to ensure the provision of core services (broadly, facilities for accepting core retail deposits, and payments and overdrafts relating to core retail deposit accounts) is separate from certain other activities within their groups, such as investment and international banking. As of 1st January 2022, the following UK banking groups are in scope of ring fencing and contain at least one ring fenced body (RFB): Barclays, HSBC, Lloyds Banking Group, NatWest group, Santander UK, TSB, and Virgin Money."

This is prudent in response to the collapse of a number of banks in 2008 following the financial crash and the massive bailout of the UK banking industry by its citizens. Since the government guarantees individual bank deposits up to £85,000, it is reasonable that banks risk their own money, and not that of retail depositors, to speculate.

As noted, the FCA works alongside the PRA in monitoring the 1500 bodies mentioned above. In addition, they regulate the conduct of around 50,000 businesses, prudentially supervise 48,000 firms, and set specific standards for around 18,000 firms.[31] It is reasonable to assume that most businesses regulated by the FCA are set up as limited liability companies, but the FCA does not monitor the financial status of these businesses; only their conduct, integrity, and market efficiency. However, to the extent that monitored financial businesses are limited liability companies, the detailed standards set for management and employees are far more than those required by the Companies Act 2006. We will consider later whether this is reasonable or whether these higher standards of the BoE, the PRA and the FCA could, at least in part, be extended to cover large, economically important limited companies.

There is some comfort from the fact that the BoE and PRA exercise relatively close monitoring of the key 1500 businesses, mainly companies, operating in the financial sector, and to a lesser degree that the FCA is monitoring the much larger number of businesses for which it is responsible. Experience has shown this to be necessary and recent scandals involving finance companies show that this will always be the case.

The IMF review (country report No 22/57) states in its introduction:

"The United Kingdom financial system enjoys a strong reputation for the quality of oversight and the design of the

---

[31] Prudential Conduct Authority website.

financial stability framework set up after the 2007-09 Global Financial Crisis.

"Ongoing structural shifts and transitional issues including: (i) the rising intermediation by non-bank financial institutions (NBFIs)...

"NBFI refers to all types of investment funds, finance companies, broker-dealers, structured finance vehicles, central counterparties, money lenders, captive funds, and bank holding companies. NBFI credit providers comprise investment funds, insurers, pension funds, money lenders, and finance companies. ... NBFIs are now sizeable credit providers to the real economy, including in riskier market niches less served by banks. They are already interconnected among themselves and with banks, including cross-border firms and asset managers ... Active use of financial technology is deepening these linkages, and data gaps preclude identification and a more definitive assessment of such risks.

"Therefore, whilst we should feel comfort that oversight is taking place, there are challenges on the horizon."[32]

Although it is not strictly relevant to the role of the limited company in the UK, it is worth noting the following extracts from the IMF report:

"The United Kingdom remains a vital global financial hub. At end-2020, the United Kingdom was by far the largest trading marketplace for credit, foreign exchange, and interest rate derivatives. U.K.-based entities are involved in 30 to 40 percent of the world's cross-border credit, currency, and interest rate derivatives contracts.

"Since the last FSAP, the U.K. financial system has grown in complexity, sophistication, and in the effective

---

[32] International Monetary Fund Country Report 22/57, February 2022.

management of financial stability. It is a system of roughly equal asset size split into banks and NBFIs.

"Although banks continue to play a central intermediation role – including through market-making, brokerage, and wholesale funding – NBFIs are also important providers of retail and corporate credit and are a core part of the United Kingdom's onshore and offshore financial system. Banks and NBFIs are interlinked through both activities and ownership structures.

"The United Kingdom financial system is central to global finance. About half of the banking sector's assets and one third of NBFIs' assets are offshore. The United Kingdom is the largest host jurisdiction to foreign financial firms as subsidiaries or branches... One-third, and sometimes even one-half, of the world's currencies and derivatives are traded and cleared in London, and most of the global broker dealers are concentrated in the United Kingdom. The United Kingdom also hosts two global systemically important CCPs (Central Clearing Counterparty) (LCH, ICE Clear), and LME Clear."[33]

It is clearly important for the citizens of the United Kingdom that this activity is closely monitored, as in 2008 the collapse of a part of it cost them billions of pounds. The final question is: is it worth it? Do the rewards equal the risks for the citizen?

"NBFIs (Non-Bank Financial Institutions) play an important role across several lending segments, including in the riskier market niches less served by banks. [Their] lending has expanded domestically and cross-border, especially in the CRE [Commercial Real Estate] and SME [Small and Medium Sized Enterprises] sectors, and in specific mortgage products and unsecured consumer credit. Some nonbank lending, such as buy-now-pay-later schemes and

---

[33] Ibid.

corporate loans, remain outside the regulatory perimeter and lack granular data for an in-depth risk analysis, including interconnectedness through key market segments [or a translation, we can't assess the risk of this lending]. Some nonbank lenders rely heavily on bank funding and on securitisations [pooling assets and selling them on], creating interlinkages with the rest of the financial system, including banks, which could amplify contagion. For instance, nearly half of funding of U.K. finance companies comes from banks. Balance sheet linkages exist with overseas banks and asset managers as well."

Often, the potential risk area is not the most obvious.

"Cloud outsourcing heightens the need for more direct supervisory attention and understanding of the underlying structures and practices. The PRA and FCA lack express statutory authority to directly review and examine any critical services from cloud and other third-party providers to regulated entities. Firms' increasing use of the cloud to perform core services raises operational (and potentially systemic) risks given the relatively small number of providers involved. The authorities should seek legislation granting direct supervisory access to third-party providers."[34]

Finally,

"As part of its international finance activities, private capital markets are also becoming a major force out of the United Kingdom for corporate and SME financing. This is routed mainly through 'alternative asset managers', who offer private equity, venture capital and private credit funding options. Data on this practice is scant, and this trend needs to be fully explored with international cooperation."[35]

---

[34] Ibid.
[35] Ibid.

This apparent digression is necessary to re-emphasise the dominant nature of finance in the UK economy and to amplify the comments by the International Monetary Fund that much of this activity is not transparent and is difficult to risk-assess. There are risks, and the potential cost to the citizen is large. A paper by the International Monetary Fund (No. 490, February 2015) considers why financial sector growth harms real growth. (See also Brookings Institute. Finance, Productivity and Distribution. October 1st 2016). The abstract of the IMF paper puts it more elegantly and talks about the "negative relationship between the rate of growth of the financial sector and the rate of growth of total factor productivity". The paper is highly technical but to quote two key passages:

"This is a consequence of the fact that financial sector growth benefits disproportionately high collateral/low productivity projects. This mechanism reflects the fact that periods of high financial sector growth often coincide with the strong development in sectors like construction, where returns on projects are relatively easy to pledge as collateral, but productivity (growth) is relatively low."

"Specifically, we find that manufacturing sectors that are either R&D-intensive or dependent on external finance suffer disproportionate reductions in productivity growth when finance booms. That is, we confirm the results in the model: by draining resources from the real economy, financial sector growth becomes a drag on real growth."[36]

Lending to the non-finance sector accounts for only 20% of bank balance sheets in the UK, with the rest accounted for by inter-bank claims. Of the total lending to non-finance firms, roughly two-thirds goes towards mortgages and of the rest the majority goes towards acquiring real-estate assets.

---

[36] International Monetary Fund (No. 490, February 2015)

The detailed analysis of the IMF appears to be perfectly mirrored in the UK.

Perhaps the greatest unquantified risk in this huge UK finance centre is in the area where it leads the world, in credit, foreign exchange and interest rate derivatives. Derivatives are contracts between parties about the future price or value of the underlying asset and are often leveraged, meaning a small movement in the underlying asset can result in a larger profit or loss on the derivative. Leverage is the use of borrowed funds (debt) to increase the potential return on an investment or project.

An example of the unexpected and potentially damaging effect of derivatives can be seen in the October 2022 panic caused in the pension industry by LDIs (Liability Driven Investments). By using leverage (borrowing), pension schemes can ensure the value of their asset portfolio moves in line with bond prices whilst holding less than 100% of the portfolio in (low return) bonds. The percentage of assets held less than 100% is decided by the degree of leverage used, with levels varying from one to seven times, but when bond prices unexpectedly fell and yields increased, a scheme with a supposedly conservative leverage of three times would be called upon for substantial collateral calls – that is, to deposit more money. At short notice, the only way to raise that money was to sell long-dated bonds and the bond market went into freefall, to be rescued by the Bank of England. Catastrophe was averted, but at great cost. The danger here was linked to leverage, and wherever derivatives are used there inevitably appears leverage.

According to the Bank for International Settlement's Statistical release: OTC (over the counter) derivatives statistics at end-December 2021, the notional amount of OTC derivatives declined modestly in the second half of 2021, to $600 trillion compared to the gross domestic product of the world at $50 trillion, and notional value of all derivatives contracts outstanding at $700 trillion, i.e. fourteen times greater than the GDP of the world! Also, the market capitalisation of every major corporation in the world adds up to about $43 trillion. Once again, the notional value of derivative contracts employed by these corporations to hedge their risks is several times their valuation, i.e., $700 trillion.

The foreign exchange or forex market is the largest financial market in the world – larger even than the stock market – with a daily volume of $6.6 trillion, according to the 2019 Triennial Central Bank Survey of FX and OTC derivatives markets.

Currency can be traded through spot transactions (exchanging one currency for another immediately), forwards (exchanging currency in the future at an agreed rate), and swaps (converting one currency obligation to another currency). Option contracts give the holder the right, but not the obligation, to buy or sell a specific currency pair at a predetermined exchange rate by a future date, where the underlying instrument is a currency. Currency trading occurs continuously around the world, twenty-four hours a day, five days a week, not always by traders who need currency for business transactions but purely as speculation.

"Derivatives are often said to provide 'zero-sum' payoffs, in the sense that there is no net gain or loss of overall monetary wealth as a result of the transaction, a derivatives contract merely redistributes pre-existing wealth. In this narrow sense, all derivatives are indeed zero-monetary-sum transactions."[37]

---

[37] Derivatives, A Twenty-First Century Understanding. 2011. Timothy E Lynch.

It could also be added that derivatives come with considerable risk, made more dangerous through often excessive leverage.

The IMF states that the UK is by far the largest trading marketplace for credit, foreign exchange and interest rate derivatives and UK-based entities are involved in thirty to forty percent of the world's cross-border credit, currency, and interest-rate derivatives contracts. Recalling the opening comment, that Britain is a finance centre with a medium-sized country attached, the citizens of the country, who are exposed financially to these risks, should be wary.

There is a question to be answered as to whether such risk levels are mitigated by secondary monitoring, the British method, or by primary control. Until the 1980s, primary control (currency exchange controls, etc) was the preferred option, and this option may have to be revisited as the complexity of the current world financial market means that regulators, according to the IMF, are in many instances flying blind, and only react to destabilising events, rather than monitoring them.

What needs to be acknowledged is that there are still important areas of the huge British finance market which require additional or new monitoring, as noted by the IMF. Non-Bank Financial Institutions are interconnected among themselves and with banks, and the use of financial technology leaves data gaps. Cloud outsourcing needs far more direct supervision. The PRA and FCA should seek legislation granting direct supervisory access to third-party providers.

The United Kingdom financial system is central to global finance and no British government should contemplate reducing the current level of supervision. Indeed, the known gaps in data access and knowledge should be addressed urgently.

Thames Water

It may seem strange to include a short diversion on the Thames Water group in the chapter covering banks and finance, but the source of business for the City of London is often debated, especially the levels of onshore and offshore business. A look at the structure of the Thames group is informative. There is one regulated company linked to two other companies, which are financially linked to the regulated company. There are then several companies between this securitisation group and the ultimate holding company.

This structure is common where a holding company or companies are set up to acquire another company. It is not uncommon for the holding company to borrow the acquisition funding with the intention of repaying the debt and interest from the profits of the acquired company. This sometimes works but if the profits are not sufficient, the acquired company can borrow to fund the acquisition.

From the Thames Water annual report for 2021 we can see that the company made an operating profit of £488.8 million, had finance expenses of £208.1 million, and a net loss on financial instruments of £522.2 million. One may well ask why a water company, supplying water to southern England and collecting sterling from the residents, would have such losses. The short answer is that the company has short-term borrowings of £1,124.9 million, long-term borrowings of £11,643.3 million, and derivative financial liabilities of £1,469.9 million. From the detailed list of borrowings, loans are in a number of currencies other than sterling. What this means is best quoted directly from the report (page 123):

"The group raises debt in a variety of currencies and uses derivative contracts to manage the foreign exchange risk exposure on this debt. The Group also uses derivative contracts to manage interest rate and inflation risk."[38]

From the financial statements of Thames Water Utilities Finance plc, there are thirty-seven secured bonds and nine loans and private placings in varying currencies. So the City of London and possibly other financial centres can be of paid assistance to one company providing water to a part of south-east England. This is in respect of audit, banking, company creation and management, legal and banking services in setting up loan agreements and other borrowing instruments, currency, interest and inflation swaps and derivatives, and a whole plethora of related services. This is just one example. The City of London can thank water-users in and around London for profitable business.

The money-go-round continues without pause. The Thames Tunnel, the super-sewer under London, should have been funded and built by Thames Water Utilities Limited, the water supplier to the south-east of England, but with its finances in a terrible state it could not fund the project. So the City of London made yet another killing when a new company, Bazalgette Tunnel Limited, was approved for the project. Used solely by Thames Water to input and output wastewater, a whole new financial pyramid was constructed, culminating in the tunnel being leased to Thames Water with, it would appear, Ofwat deciding on the lease repayment terms. If you trawl carefully through the accounts of Thames Water, you can discover that wastewater network assets are assumed to have a useful life of 150 years. At a cost of £4.2 billion, over 120 years (the official assumed life) and divided by 13,800,000 consumers, the additional cost would be £2.50 per annum. Let's be generous and make it £3, to cover finance and other costs. Currently, the proudly announced additional bill to

---

[38] Thames Water, Annual Report, 2021.

consumers is around £25 per annum, presumably to write the cost off over about 20 years. Either this must reduce rapidly in future years, or the leasing company will make a killing.

The financialization of water (and other utilities) to the consumer has become a scandal. Following the financial collapse of 2008/9, the British Government could have borrowed at close to 0% and gone a long way to rebuilding Britain's infrastructure, had utilities been nationalised.

Private utilities, in particular water, neglected renewal and borrowed heavily to pay dividends to, usually, offshore owners. It is the citizen/consumer who carries this excess cost whilst enriching the owners of finance and other companies.

Chapter 5
A British Company Overview

It is remarkably easy to create a company in the UK. The responsibility for registering new companies and monitoring compliance with the rules on filing information about the company and supplying financial statements at the required time is the responsibility of Companies House, an Executive Agency of the Department for Business, Energy and Industrial Strategy (BEIS). It is funded by income from fees, but penalties collected when financial statements are filed late are paid to HM Treasury.

The number of companies incorporated in the United Kingdom is staggering. At the end of March 2022 there were 4.9 million incorporated companies on the register of Companies House. Excluding those in dissolution or liquidation, the number is still enormous, at 4.5 million. Even more remarkable is the growth in the number of companies in the last forty years. Between 1979 and 2022, the total register increased by 4.1 million companies, whilst the effective register increased by 3.8 million. This overall growth has been matched by the number of companies being added to and removed from the register on an annual basis. Between April 2021 and March 2022, there were 753,000 company incorporations and in the same period 581,000 dissolutions.

Without doubt, these numbers were inflated by the effects of the Covid pandemic, but the number of incorporations and dissolutions over time has increased at a steady rate. This means that around one fifth of companies are registered and removed from the register each year. It is beyond the scope of this book to assess the effect on society of a situation where it is as easy to form a limited company as it is to get a library card, and far easier than obtaining a credit card.

The average age of UK companies on the total register in 2021/2022 was 8.6 years, and over half of the companies were aged under five years, whilst over two-thirds were less than ten years old. A mere one in ten companies were aged over twenty years. This is not a new phenomenon; the average age of companies in the UK has always been relatively young. Examining the types of company included in the register, private limited companies account for around 96% of all companies registered. Clearly, the low capital requirement and the ease of creation have contributed to an explosion in private limited companies, but in contrast public limited companies have been declining in number since 2008 and now, at 5951, account for only 0.1% of all companies.

To examine in more depth the make-up of these companies, one must turn to the Business Population Estimates[39], which show that there were 5.5 million private sector businesses in the United Kingdom at the start of 2022, made up of:

- 5.47 million small businesses (0 to 49 employees)
- 35,900 medium-sized businesses (50 to 249 employees)
- 7,700 large businesses (250 or more employees)

These businesses employ in total 27 million people but the number of businesses employing staff (in addition to the owner) is 1.4 million, or 26.3% of the total, and these businesses employ 23 million people (84% of the total employees). The vast majority of these businesses are

---

[39] Department for Business, Energy and Industrial Strategy. Business Population Estimates for the UK and Regions. 6th October 2022.

incorporated as companies (including public corporations and nationalised bodies) and number 1.1 million businesses, with 21 million (78%) employees.

Having seen that most businesses employing staff in the United Kingdom are incorporated companies, the next stage is to establish the breakdown of employment by the size of company. Certain data is not analysed in the records, as it is deemed to disclose too much information, but this does not prevent the calculation of employees and turnover by company size within certain bands. The data can be extracted and summarised as:

Company	Employees (million)	Employees %
50 and above	13	62
200 and above	11	49
500 and above	9	41

These data are important to our examination of the role of the limited liability company in the UK; they clarify the importance of the company to both employment and wealth generation and show how many people have a relationship with one or more companies other than as a consumer.

It is difficult to view the around one million companies with no employees other than the owner, or the 1.1 million companies with under fifty employees, as requiring the same level of regulation and monitoring as the larger companies which may have a material economic or social effect on society. Our concern with this smaller group is more in relation to the ease of creation and dissolution and the ensuing churn along with the dangers of the 'prepack' and the damage to society and individuals on a smaller scale.

Because they represent a considerable level of employment and wealth creation in the economy, companies could be grouped into employment numbers over fifty, over 200, and over 500, for different levels of regulation and monitoring, but to avoid the possibility of artificial suppression of employee numbers, most of these limitations will also have to apply to groups of companies employing more than these numbers of employees.

The increase in the number of private companies and the decrease in public limited companies and companies quoted on the London Stock Exchange has a variety of causes. A report by the University of Edinburgh Business School[40] suggested there are four, including company assets rebalancing towards intangibles, public companies facing higher costs than private companies, and investors increasing focus on short-term returns. Only the first of these three is relatively new.

The fourth reason was also relatively new, and significant: the growth in private equity funds. To avoid the accusation of exaggerating the effect of this phenomenon, it is best to quote Bain and Co, who describe themselves as the leading consultancy partner in the private equity industry.

"The flow of capital into the private markets is unprecedented. Global financial capital increased 53% from 2000 to 2010, reaching some $600 trillion, or 10 times real global GDP. Bain's Macro Trends Group projects that it is swelling by half again and will reach approximately $900 trillion by the end of 2020.

"This age of superabundance has had both negative and positive effects. The flood of capital led to the housing and buyout booms that imploded so spectacularly during the global financial crisis.... Since the start of the current economic cycle in 2009, investors have allocated a staggering

---

[40] Report by the University of Edinburgh Business School for the All-Party Parliamentary Corporate Governance Group. October 2020.

$5.8 trillion globally to private equity [private equity is an investment class where private companies raise capital to acquire and manage other private companies or take public companies private, with the goal of ultimately selling them for a profit] and the debt markets have been eager to finance such transactions.

"Taken to the extreme, this pattern would end up placing most cash-generating companies in private hands. Public ownership in that case would be reserved for companies that must exist in the public realm for regulatory reasons (banks, insurance companies, utilities) or because they can't carry leverage [high levels of borrowing].The median holding period [how long funds are holding onto companies before selling them] fell 10% last year to 4.5 years, after edging down slowly from a peak of 5.9 years in 2014."[41]

Because of this phenomenon, not all the private companies incorporated during the creation boom are small- or medium-sized companies. Many are large companies; some former public companies converted to private companies, some created by private equity putting together smaller companies or setting up chains of holding companies to hold debt, often incurred as part of acquisition. Edinburgh University Business School notes that one disadvantage for public companies is: "Private equity funds appear to benefit from preferential tax treatment because of the way they are financed. Funds can finance their purchases through debt, and this provides them with a tax shield because, unlike dividends, interest is tax deductible."[42]

This is a clear indication that private companies can extract untaxed profits, sometimes offshore.

---

[41] Global Private Equity Report. 2019. Bain and Co.
[42] Ibid.

Companies with more than 200 employees employ 49% of employed people, excluding the approximately 5.5 million micro business and those with over 500 employees (41%). These are important data and will be relevant when we consider employment law and the remuneration of employees by companies.

Is there 'quid pro quo', in the form of remuneration, training and safety, which society requires for the benefit of setting up a limited liability company?

Identifying the Problems

Chapter 6
The State or the Market (Markets)

"States are often complicit in the creation of the market as authoritative. When state leaders proclaim the forces of the global market give them little room to manoeuvre or independent policy choice, they are participating in the construction of the market as authoritative. They are not only ceding claims of authority to the market, but they are also creating the authority of the market."
The Emergence of Private Authority in Global Governance
Rodney Bruce Hall and Thomas Biersteker (eds) 2002

The historic justification for the high rewards to the capitalist were for the risk of engaging his capital in a venture with the possibility that it might all be lost. This ended with the introduction of the limited liability company.

Companies are not necessary for capitalism to function; it functioned in overdrive at the end of the 18th century and the first half of the 19th century, when joint stock companies with limited liability were prohibited in the United Kingdom, and throughout the 19th century, when limited liability had not yet finally been defined.

Limited liability companies are one of many legal structures available to manage asset ownership and should have no preferential place in the economic sphere.

The limited liability company has enabled great wealth to accumulate. Before this development, failure or decline usually cost the capitalist his or her accumulated capital. After, losses and damage could be 'ring fenced' and pushed on to someone else, with all earlier gains protected. Risk is removed, or is capable of being removed, from capitalism.

Companies are equally at home in a dictatorship or a democracy. China has seen a big expansion in privately-owned companies, with many Chinese businesspeople growing extraordinarily rich. Mussolini's definition of fascism was the merger of a militarist state with corporate power and by this definition we may soon have to reclassify China from a communist state to a proto-fascist state. This is a worrying development as company managements are often happy to work with a dictatorial or even fascist state, often preferring one to a democratic state.

The downside for the capitalist is that fascist states can be very unpredictable, and a false step (not necessarily a legal step) could result at best in the loss of all assets, at worst, banishment or execution. By far the best environment for the capitalist is a democracy where all effective controls over the running of a company (social, environmental and financial) have been removed but where the rule of law is secure enough to protect assets. This is the libertarian ideology pursued by sections of US business and their supporters and is the true meaning of the worst aspects of 'globalisation' as seen over the last forty years; it is still the goal of certain sectors in society. We should look at how socially and economically useful structures can suddenly become dangerous due to changes in the political and technical environment, having repercussions that were never expected or, by most citizens, desired.

The juxtaposition of the limited liability company locking out future penalties for failure, or even fraud, alongside the ending of all exchange controls, and the development of the internet and immediate world-wide connectivity, placed a power in the hands of capital which it could never have dreamed of. The challenge is for the citizen to regain control over the company as the worldwide web cannot be un-invented and, although in some circumstances exchange controls may be necessary, the reintroduction of worldwide exchange controls, as with the Bretton Woods system, is unlikely.

In 1944 at Bretton Woods, New Hampshire, United States representatives from all the leading allied states collectively founded a regulated system of fixed exchange rates, indirectly linked to the US dollar and tied to gold. The system collapsed in 1971 when the United States suspended the dollar's convertibility to gold, with its official abolition in 1973.

In a rare moment of transparency for a senior military figure, in 1935 US Major-General Smedley-Butler confessed, relating to events going back almost to 1900: "I spent 33 years and four months in active military service and during that period I spent most of my time as a high-class muscle man for Big Business, for Wall Street and the bankers. In short, I was a racketeer, a gangster for capitalism. I helped make Mexico and especially Tampico safe for American oil interests in 1914. I helped make Haiti and Cuba a decent place for the National City Bank boys to collect revenues in. I helped in the raping of half a dozen Central American republics for the benefit of Wall Street. I helped purify Nicaragua for the International Banking House of Brown Brothers in 1902-1912. I brought light to the Dominican Republic for the American sugar interests in 1916. I helped make Honduras right for the American fruit companies in 1903. In China in 1927 I helped see to it that Standard Oil went on its way unmolested. Looking back on it, I might have given Al Capone a few hints. The best he could do was to operate his racket in three districts. I operated on three continents."

It would be quite possible to attribute this quote to 2025 as the veil which until now had been cast over predatory capitalism has been lifted and is laid bare for all to see.

A Recent Rapid Breakdown

Recent events have shown in a quite brutal fashion that the choice not to exercise the immense power of the state is a political one, which can be changed in an instant if it is deemed necessary. Suddenly, the reality of a nation state's potential power becomes clear. Sanctions have been applied by countries many times in the recent past but on countries where the effects have not registered greatly in the West. Now, following the invasion of a new and fledgling democratic state, Ukraine, the speed and ferocity of state power over individuals and business, including companies, is revealed. Whilst fully justified, this gives the lie to the oft-repeated line that countries can do little in the face of corporate power. This terrible event has exposed the weak legal framework in the United Kingdom in respect of companies, the already noted weaknesses of Companies House and the registering of companies, but also the weakness in the bodies intended to monitor and control them.

It is easiest to deal first with the sanctions imposed by the United Kingdom. One of the major planks of the economic crime bill now passed by Parliament is that in theory it should be impossible for Russian individuals to own property in the United Kingdom by means of an offshore company. Informed commentators, in particular Oliver Bullough, have demonstrated the ease with which this can be circumvented.

We have previously seen that because Companies House is unable to carry out checks on the details provided during the formation of a company, it is probably easier to hold the property through a United Kingdom company. Certainly, it is much cheaper. We must conclude therefore that although the United Kingdom has the power to take action against an undesirable foreigner using a United Kingdom company, it has neither the will nor committed the necessary finance to make this happen.

How have the two economic powers most prepared to exercise their power, the United States and the European Union, fared? Globalisation was once claimed to be a means of reducing conflict, by creating a web of dependencies which would bring former enemies closer economically. This vision must now be in doubt.

It is difficult to overestimate the economic power of the United States. Its power derives from the US Dollar, the most widely used currency for trade and financial transactions, with a United States bank often involved. It is therefore difficult for financial institutions (aka financial companies, banks), central banks and many other companies to operate when cut off from the United States financial system. Sanctions on this scale, particularly against a central bank, have been used in the past but against countries and companies not widely integrated into international commerce, such as North Korea and Iran. For the first time, wide-ranging financial sanctions have been initiated against a large country integrated into the worldwide trading system; that is, one involved in globalisation. Western sanctions, mainly United States sanctions, on Russia's central bank have reduced its ability to support the Russian economy and largely neutralised the country's foreign currency reserves.

The point of this exercise in financial power is to 'de-globalise' the Russian economy, to shut out its banks and companies from the 'global' economy. The integration of the large Russian market has presented huge challenges for a large number of Western companies with extensive and often profitable operations in Russia. They are now faced with the power of the 'state', often claimed to be powerless in the face of major, globally present companies. The truth is clear; these companies are powerless and have only two options: remain in Russia and risk a backlash, or get out. Almost without exception they 'got out', and quickly, or at the very least limited new investment, or mothballed activity. This dilemma presents a particular problem when companies produce foodstuffs, medicines or other products which can be considered essential to life.

Do other countries have to comply with sanctions imposed by the United States? Most Western countries will comply in any event, but question marks remain in respect of countries which are trading globally but not necessarily as part of the Western consensus. China trades extensively with Russia and continues to do so but is wary of incurring United States sanctions, certainly in respect of goods which may aid a war effort.

India has the same dilemma, having extensive ties with Russia but requiring raw materials and other supplies. Direct threats of action if India breaks sanctions have not yet been uttered publicly by the United States.

The other economic power large enough to effectively sanction Russia is the European Union. Unlike the United States, many countries within the European Union have close economic ties to Russia and their companies have substantial investments in that country. As sanctions have two ends, the sanctioned and the sanctioner, the potential economic damage to companies within Europe is substantial, both directly in respect of trade and indirectly, should Europe cease to import much of its oil and gas from Russia. European Union sanctions have targeted individuals and Russian companies but the exodus of European multi-national companies from Russia has been voluntary.

"The Berlin Government has seized control of Gazprom Germania, the subsidiary of the Russian gas group which operates some of Germany's largest natural gas storage facilities ... Gazprom Germania GmbH operates critical infrastructure in Germany and so has huge significance for the gas supply." The United Kingdom is also not without its troubles as Gazprom Germania is the parent company of Gazprom Marketing and Trading, headquartered in the UK, and the Russian group's global trading wing. One step further down the chain, its UK retail division Gazprom Energy supplies about a fifth of business gas to commercial customers. Most countries will now be taking a critical look at the security of supply and control over essential natural resources and their infrastructure.

Sanctions against individuals often make the headlines, but it is sanctions against companies which do the real economic damage. Probably the most effective sanction initiated within – but not directly by – the European Union was the suspension of SWIFT access to certain Russian banks, freezing at least temporarily their ability to transact with the rest of the world.

The notification of this act is interesting in that as a company, SWIFT makes clear it is following a directive and has no choice in the matter.

"Diplomatic decisions taken by the European Union, in consultation with the United Kingdom, Canada and the United States, bring SWIFT into efforts to end this crisis by requiring us to disconnect select Russian banks from our financial messaging services. As previously stated, we will fully comply with applicable sanctions laws. To this end, in compliance with the Legal Instructions in EU Council Regulation (EU)2022/345 of 1 March 2022, we will disconnect seven designated Russian entities (and their designated Russian based subsidiaries) from the SWIFT network."

The clearly legal nature of this communication is to avoid legal claims for breach of contract. What is interesting here is that SWIFT is incorporated under Belgian law, and one would therefore expect Belgium to legislate for sanction rules. Neither the European Union nor the United States controls SWIFT, but a European Union directive has caused SWIFT to act against its members.

We are clearly here extending the power of the state over companies to encompass the power of the European Union over companies. This is relevant when we exhort the European Union to act on behalf of its citizens in other areas; clearly it has the capacity.

Throughout this book, I suggest that countries have the power to legislate in respect of companies to any extent they consider necessary but choose, in general, not to do so. It is now clear that not only countries, but also the European Union, have extensive power in this regard. It is remarkable how quickly globalisation can be reversed by the nation state and the European Union when they consider it important to do so. Suddenly the real power of government is apparent. As also is the need to constantly review who controls critical resources and infrastructure. Who does so is not an irrelevance.

We have already noted the ability of states to project power to provide access to markets for corporate interests but recent events, as we have already seen in the case of the war in Ukraine, have again provided clear evidence that the claim by democratic state politicians that in the face of the 'market' they are unable to hold companies to account is simply hollow rhetoric.

Chapter 7
Employment

Company law cannot enforce behavioural or detailed standards of employment and so must limit itself to preventing abuse or unfair treatment of company employees, who can also lay claim to being the fellow citizens of those in management who are tasked with training and supporting them. It is, however, legitimate to expect company law to have broad limitations on a company management's ability to behave unfairly or injuriously towards fellow workers, or limit their right to self-expression or association.

Much of our management thinking has been influenced by Frederick Winslow Taylor, an American born in 1856 and best known for his work at Bethlehem Steel, where his organisational efforts doubled efficiency. There was, however, a dark side to Taylor's approach as he did not expect workers to think; this was the job of management. Workers were no different to machines and were expendable. Taylor dehumanised labour and indirectly this led to the cult of the strong leader; if no-one else is thinking, the strong leader must do the thinking for all. This in turn bred something else – fear – and many companies had a fear culture, not dependent on aggression or rudeness but on a lack of trust. Fortunately, these attitudes are no longer fashionable in management circles but, owing to the hierarchal nature of most company organisations, have not completely disappeared. This was more so in Britain because of the familiarity with which people are addressed compared to many countries in Europe. This apparent familiarity hides a remnant of the old master-servant relationship in higher levels of management. This would be understood as impolite, demeaning and unacceptable in many continental countries.

The role of top management in any company is to supply resources and direction and to define strategy. Middle management's role is to deploy that strategy and to establish and maintain standards. Supervisors take part in and encourage small group activities. All these groups have a duty to build an environment in which people can realise their full potential through mutual trust, respect, and support. They must also set up agreed goals and measures at every level of the organisation and ensure that individual goals are consistent with the overall aims of the organisation. To do this they need data and structured problem-prevention tools.[43]

Managers and senior managers often lack detailed knowledge of business processes and any change they introduce may well be based on ignorance of detail. Top-down change may be unencumbered by facts, and there is every reason for company management to encourage employees, often with intimate knowledge of process, to suggest better ways of doing things and to give them respect for their achievements and their ability to think, challenge and innovate.

This philosophy is not currently reflected in company law and can only be to a limited extent. This is not the case when it comes to placing a true value on the contribution of employees in tangible terms.

---

[43] Breaking Down Barriers, Devlin and Hand, 1993

Valuing labour

A limited liability company is nothing more than the people who are employed by it. One may also wish to include people who interact with it but who are not employees, such as outside consultants and professionals or those who are employed by the state. The success of any company, however, can only be the result of the efforts of its employees, from top to bottom. Remove all humans from Marks & Spencer or Jaguar-Land Rover and what do you have? Silent buildings, silent machinery, and a mass of totally useless assets capable of producing nothing.

This is an interesting subject and may well be worth a book in its own right (pace Ricardo and Marx). At the very simplest, given that the company is a creation of multiple contracts, to have any relationship with the company, an employee must have a contract. So far so good. But the power relationship between an employee and the company is unbalanced, both directly and indirectly, in that the managing director of a major company may (currently) well have direct access to government in order to be able to direct legislation, whereas the employee as individual citizen can vote every five years for a pre-prepared and non-binding manifesto.

Marx defined class in relation to the structure (that is, one's position within it) of production. This concept is still relevant in defining the allocation of wealth (profit, excess production, or however you wish to term it) between capital and labour. Nowhere is this clearer than in the division of 'profit' within a company.

What remains true in the labour theory of value is that in general only labour can add value. The proof of this is that when labour is withdrawn, production stops. It does not stop at once because value is locked up in machinery and assets so that today, unlike in Marx's day, robots in a factory could conceivably keep functioning and producing, at least until they broke down or needed servicing. When worn out, they would need labour to reproduce them. So, the basis of all production is labour.

Skill and scarcity mean that today many participants in the labour market are satisfied enough with their income not to cease working in order to increase it. Some workers, however, and it is difficult to identify exactly how many, have so low an income that they are poor, some even needing the additional support of the state to prevent poverty.

A question to be asked is whether it is legitimate to use the opportunity presented by permitting the formation of limited liability companies to insist that as a quid pro quo, as a minimum all employees (directly or indirectly, so including agency workers) of limited liability companies should be paid a 'living income' (not the current living wage, which is a renamed minimum wage)?

If so, should all companies have to do this, or only those over a specific size, or with a minimum number of employees? We have already agreed that the company is a necessity and not an instrument of exploitation but, in the interest of justice and fairness, why not guarantee this?

Current economic theory would appear to suggest that companies are doing individuals (citizens) a favour by employing them. The truth is that they must employ or die, and the reason strikes are so feared is that they at once demonstrate how dependent all limited liability companies are on their employees.

A guaranteed living wage paid by companies would prevent the state having to subsidise large, profitable companies, but would not prevent the state from continuing to support individuals if necessary.

According to the figures companies with more than 200 employees accounted for over 11 million people in employment nationally (49%). Those employing more than 500 accounted for 9.3 million people (41%). Profitable companies within a range to be set between these levels could well legitimately be expected to pay a living wage. For most, this would not present a major burden, and would relieve the state of a level of unjustified subsidy to that limited number of companies who abuse state support for individuals.

Protecting the Whistleblower

A new companies act should also include clauses which fully protect employees and directors from any retaliation should they report illegal activity by another employee or director to the relevant authorities.

As a name on a piece of paper, a company itself cannot carry out an illegal activity; only an individual acting under the authority of the company can do this. Reaching back to the controls and risk assessments recommended by the Bank of England, all companies should have structures in place, relative to their size, to minimise the risk of illegal activity. A blueprint as to how such legislation could be drafted is available in the EU Directive on Whistleblowers.

Britain has, for historical reasons, an unfair view of reporting company-related crime. The following extract from the British Government is extraordinary in the detail it goes into in respect of benefit fraud:

Reporting a crime | The Crown Prosecution Service. If you witness a crime, you have a vital role to play in bringing the criminals to justice.

Report someone you think is committing benefit fraud.

Give as much information as you can about the person you're reporting. This could include:
- their name
- their address
- the type of fraud you think they're committing

You can make a report anonymously - you do not have to give your name or contact details unless you want to.[44]

The observant reader will see at once that the citizen is encouraged to report benefit fraud and is given anonymity and an address to contact. Although the government provides opportunity to report corporate tax evasion, environmental law breaches, or other corporate crimes, this does not seem to be widely used.

This despite the fact that corporate tax crime amounts to losses to the state much greater than those caused by benefit fraud. The reason for this is understandable, given that in the current state of the law a whistle-blower would be in considerable danger of retaliation.

The world is still waiting for the time when, at least once, a company's management accepts immediately that a serious error or accident has occurred and offers an apology along with a clear commitment to try to mitigate or make good the

---

[44] GOV.UK Home Crime, justice and the law
Reporting crimes - GOV.UK https://www.gov.uk/browse/justice/reporting-crimes 1 of 3 06/11/2023,) Report benefits fraud (/report-benefit-fraud

damage. What causes rational and moral individuals to appear to lose all these virtues when they become senior corporate managers?

Further down the management chain, fear is the overriding factor as the middle manager who urged admission and contrition would never work again, but is this true of top management? Are they fearful for their jobs, now and in the future, or does corporate life, involving the aggressive climb up the greasy pole, lead to an irrational sense of loyalty to a legal fiction?

Years ago, I was talking to a Scottish engineer about his work. He told me of an incident he had been involved in along with several colleagues, working on a production plant in Europe during its annual servicing. A serious accident had happened. The plant had not been shut down correctly and a blow-out threw all the men off the facility a considerable distance to the ground. All were injured, one seriously.

The next day, when the management of the world-famous company carrying out the work appeared to check on progress, all those men were present and working, the seriously injured one strapped to a chair. The engineer explained that, had they reported the accident and initiated a health and safety review to prevent a similar incident occurring again, the tight service schedule would have been extended, costing the company money, and none of the men involved would ever have worked in the industry again; they would have appeared on a blacklist.

It is difficult to overestimate the challenges facing the EU with its directive on whistleblowing, or the challenge facing a revised companies act containing protection for citizens performing their civic duty, i.e. whistleblowers.

When considering the duty of a citizen to protect his or her fellow citizens from harm, could a timely exposure of lax health and safety practices or inadequate maintenance at Bhopal in India, were this in fact the case, have saved the lives of over 20,000 people, and saved thousands more from long-term health damage?

It is probably not the case that sufficient information was available to save thousands of children from Thalidomide damage, but why is it necessary for companies to avoid or delay compensation for as long as possible?

The answer is simple and is included in the Companies Act 2006: the overriding duty of company management is to their shareholders (owners).

As a citizen in a democracy, you have the right to expect that those entrusted with running companies should obey the law, take every measure to ensure the safety of their employees and the public, and, should something go amiss, alert all concerned and take immediate action to minimise any damage. Should they not do this, you have a duty to your fellow citizens to expose this fact as soon as possible. You are expected to do this in the case of benefit fraud. How much more important is it in the case of real risk or damage?

Britain has comprehensive legal protections for employees, initiated both by the UK government and by the European Union. Substantial laws were already in place on equal pay, maternity rights, sex, disability and race discrimination, and health and safety, added to by laws that resulted from European Union Directives including around sexual orientation, age and religion or belief discrimination, and these are generally well embedded. British governments, however, strongly resisted laws on equal treatment rights for agency workers, working-time limits, and the right for workers to receive information and be consulted on workplace changes which could affect their jobs or terms and conditions. It is still to be seen if Britain leaving the European Union results in the dilution of any of these rights, beyond the obvious ones such as the removal of the right to belong to a European Works Council.

Perhaps in rewriting the companies act, the first major principle to be proposed should be the fair and equal treatment of all employees. Although it is possible in Britain for a director not to be an employee, in practice this is rare and everyone in a company is an employee with an employment contract, regardless of their official title within the hierarchy. A company therefore has possibly thousands of employees who are residents and mostly citizens of Britain, all doing important jobs; otherwise, why employ them?

Seen in this light, the commonality of interest amongst this group is clear. Many will have spent ten, twenty or thirty years with the company, usually the lower and middle levels longest, learning and relearning skills and assuming responsibilities and cumulatively being responsible for the success of the company.

It is instructive that a shareholder who may have acquired shares just the previous week is considered to have an important voice in matters relating to the company, its sale, closure, break-up or complete redirection, but that a long-standing employee who is not a director/employee has none.

Clearly, there are times when companies experience severe financial and other problems, sometimes caused by technological change, geographic change or legal change, which impacts the business model. Sometimes companies cease to be viable and are liquidated. For large companies which can dominate the economy of an area, this presents a major problem for the employees and local citizens. There are also cases where perfectly financially healthy and successful companies are closed or moved, to provide a financial benefit to the shareholders. In both cases, fairness demands a solution, although the method may differ.

Access to information

The first requirement should be transparency towards all employees; not necessarily in full detail but at least an overview of the challenges and proposed solutions. Some of the financial information will be available publicly, at least for the recent past, but we have seen how difficult it can be to analyse the true financial position of a group of inter-related companies, particularly if part of a private group. If changes are not the result of financial pressure but relate to technology or location, there is even less reason to withhold it. Without existing and tried formal structures, such an exercise would be difficult, if not impossible, to conduct. With whom would management talk?

For this reason, large companies need a formal structure whereby the mass of employees can consult with, and be consulted by, the shareholders.

Why do I say shareholders and not senior management, or the board of directors? Because they are acting in the name of, and for the interest of, the shareholders, whose decisions may be changed by the results of consultation and discussion.

Financial liabilities

An adequately capitalised company will be able to meet its liabilities to its employees, to the state and to its creditors.

What should those liabilities be? A competently redrafted company law would redefine the hierarchy of creditors of a company and should reinstate many of the old positions removed over recent years. Highest on the list of liabilities should be all outstanding wages and salaries and a social plan for employees, providing financial compensation depending on the number of years worked.

All taxes owing to the citizens of the country would be next. VAT held by the company, along with employees' National Insurance, never belonged to the company. This money belongs to the citizens who contribute it, and is only held by the company on their behalf. Being unable to meet that liability is tantamount to fraud.

The tax liability of the company should be met if possible and only then could a fixed and floating charge on the assets of the company be exercised.

Chapter 8
Corporate Crimes Lead to Change

The limited liability company is neither a force for good nor for evil. It is a tool which is wielded by its management, seldom by its shareholders, and if productive and compliant with the laws of the land it can be of benefit to its country of residence. It is also capable of tremendous damage, to individuals and to society. This statement, regrettably, can be shown to be true following horrific events on an unimaginable scale in the 20th century.

The limited liability company exists as a legal construction only. What does this really mean? Taking British and United States companies as examples often requires extensive and challenging explanation, but the purely legal nature of the company is best illustrated in continental Europe, damaged in the 19th and 20th centuries by war, and political and social chaos.

The names of Bayer and BASF stand out today as giants of the chemical and pharmaceutical industries, with a history dating back into the mid-19th century. What is so striking about these companies is that they existed and waxed and waned throughout a wide variety of political climates, from autocratic monarchy into democratic republicanism followed by fascism, and finally again into democratic republicanism. What is the common thread?

Both companies, Friederich Bayer and Company near Cologne and the Badische Anilin and Soda Fabrik (BASF), in Ludwigshafen on the Rhine, can trace their formation to the 1860s; as can all the chemical companies founded around this time, including household names such as Agfa, Kalle and Hoechst. They grew and prospered, driven by their entrepreneurial founders and by the many young, highly educated and motivated chemists produced by German universities at this time.

"By the early 1870s, companies like BASF, Hoechst and even struggling Bayer had snatched control of the industry from England and France and were racing away into an unassailable lead."[45]

In the period up to the turn of the 20th century, these companies discovered and patented a huge number of new chemical processes and drugs beneficial to mankind. Leading Bayer was Carl Duisberg, while BASF was headed by Heinrich Brunck and Hoechst by Gustav von Bruning. Another name which was to recur in this story was Carl Bosch of BASF, who was credited with converting the academic Fritz Haber's method of producing liquid ammonia into large-scale industrial production; the Haber-Bosch process.

The role of the German chemical industry in the Great War was not dissimilar to that of similar industries in the combatant countries; to maximise the output of offensive weapons. The war was an industrial war, carried out on an industrial scale, but on the German side marred by the first use of poison gas, initiated by Fritz Haber and supplied by BASF.

"Any reservations about the use of chemical weapons seemed to be felt more by Germany's soldiers than by her scientists. Few people epitomised the strengthening links between the chemical industry and military more than Carl Duisberg. The war was for him a turning point. In September 1916, along with Gustav Krupp, Duisberg was called to a private conference with the chief of the High Command, von Hindenburg, and his deputy, Ludendorff. "Again, Duisberg dominated the discussion... The occupied

---

[45] Hitler's Cartel, Diarmuid Jeffreys, Bloomsbury Publishing, 2008.

territories would have to be tapped for workers. In November 1916, as a direct consequence of Duisberg's remarks, the kaiser's troops began deportations from occupied Belgium – in essence, the start of a slave labour programme. In under a month, more than sixty thousand men were taken from their homes and workplaces at gunpoint and loaded onto trains for transport to factories and mines in the Reich."[46]

The efforts of the German military and industrialists were fruitless. On November 11th 1918, the armistice ended the war and began the victorious allies' mission to extract reparations from Germany. The important role played by the German chemical industry during the war was clear, and the French in particular were determined to reduce its influence and power. Carl Bosch represented the German chemical industry at the Versailles conference in 1919 (Carl Duisberg having refused), at which the Allies wished to see the complete dismantling of this industry.

This would have meant disaster for the industry, so Bosch held secret meetings with French officials and agreed to share secret technology with them in return for saving the plants. This ploy was successful, but the German chemical industry still had to give up many of its patents to Allied companies and share its markets with foreign competitors. The years immediately following the armistice were difficult for the German chemical industry, with France occupying large parts of the Ruhr and tensions running high.

Against this background, and against the odds, a weak but viable democratic republic was created in Germany with Friedrich Ebert as president, but the government was not helped by the febrile political atmosphere, with recurring attempted uprisings from both left and right. The history of the Weimar Republic is sometimes interpreted to imply that

---

[46] Hitler's Cartel, Diarmuid Jeffreys, Bloomsbury Publishing, 2008.

its failure was inevitable, but this was never the case.

The hyperinflation of the early 1920s, the loss or sharing of international markets, and the continued occupation of parts of Germany by the French led the leaders of the major German chemical companies to complete a merger that had first been mooted many years earlier by Carl Duisberg. On December 9th 1925, eight companies merged and the new company took the name of I.G. Farbenindustrie Aktiengesellschaft (I.G. Farben for short).

Robert S Yavner noted four books published before he was writing in 1984, documenting the history of I.G. Farben: The Riddle of the Rhine (1923) by Victor Lefebure, I.G. Farben (1947) by Richard Sasuly, The Devil's Chemists (1952) by Josiah Dubois, and The Crime and Punishment of I.G. Farben (1978) by Joseph Borkin to which can be added Diarmuid Jeffreys' Hitler's Cartel (2008). There has, therefore, been extensive and detailed public analysis of the history and development of these companies and the individuals involved. The dominance of I.G. Farben over the German industrial landscape is both beyond the scope of this narrative and not relative to the story. Sufficient to say that it was dominant, as controlling monopoly was not high on the German government's agenda.

Richard Sasuly compared the leaders of I.G. Farben to men like General Erich Ludendorff, who looked at the armistice which ended the First World War as no more than a suspension of hostilities. He wrote that the military and industrial leaders of Germany came out of one war entirely prepared to start thinking about another. (Yavner, 1984)

And the reader will have noted at this early point that a few names keep recurring; something to keep in mind as we progress.

1929 was the year of the financial crash, beginning in the United States and spreading around the world, piling even greater pressure on the weak German democracy. Under Bosch and influenced by Duisberg, what was the position of the group I.G. Farben in relation to the fractious and dangerous politics of the period? Almost certainly the same as that of similar heads of large groups in most countries at most times.

"Domestically, the company wanted stable government that didn't interfere in its affairs, low taxes, low inflation, limits on the power of organised labour and support for agriculture, the main consumer of its synthetic nitrate output." (Jeffreys)

This palate of requirements meant that support for the social democrats was unlikely; only centre-right, business-friendly parties were worth actively supporting. The Chemical Industry Association, chaired by Duisberg up to 1924 and by Bosch from 1927 to 1933, was active in lobbying government and civil servants.

The rise of the national socialists under Adolf Hitler is well documented and need not be repeated here. We will have to touch on the relationship between national socialism and I.G. Farben and its leading management figures, but it is not the theme of this chapter.

What is relevant, and of great importance, is the obsession of one man, a brilliant chemist, who also happened to head up the largest industrial combine in Germany. Carl Bosch. Bosch wished to develop and perfect the production of synthetic oils and fuel, which at that time was not an irrational goal, as the world was only aware of limited oil reserves and believed that these would soon be exhausted. Any company which could perfect this process and patent the method would make a fortune. The downside to the plan was that research in this field was slow, and cripplingly expensive. Throughout the late 1920s and into the early 1930s, the management of the group had supported the development, but the cost was now causing them to have second thoughts. If Bosch was to see his dream achieved, he would need a plan. The plan was to seek subvention from the German government on the basis that Germany needed a ready supply of oil for national security reasons.

Under normal circumstances this would be a major step but, with a collapsing democracy in Germany and the increasing power and influence of the fascist party, it was an extremely dangerous one. The decision by Bosch coincided with the rise to power of the national socialists and inevitably brought the management of I.G. Farben into contact with the leaders of the fascist movement. That interaction went as far as Bosch arranging through an intermediary a meeting between Hitler and some of I.G.'s chemists expert in synthetic oil development, at which Hitler showed a keen interest in the technology.

The future direction was set.

"By the end of 1933, the IG had handed over RM4.5million in contributions to one [national socialist] fund or another... To solidify Farben's position in the new regime, Hermann Schmitz (now a board member) was appointed an honorary Nazi deputy in the Reichstag on 28 November 1933. Buetefisch joined the SS and became a member of Heinrich Himmler's Circle of Friends... I.G. Farben was an active, indispensable, and often enthusiastic ally of Hitler. Out of ambition, dislike, and a fear of communism, the Farben directors saw the Nazis as both their opportunity and their protection. After the Second World War, Georg von Schnitzler admitted that Nazi foreign policy and I.G. Farben's foreign policy were largely inseparable. Arthur Schweitzer, in Big Business in the Third Reich, described the Four-Year Plan (1936) as a joint project of the Nazis, the leading generals in the Ministry of War, and I.G. Farben, who together formed a new relationship in economic matters." (Yavner)

In December 1933, the management of I.G. Farben signed a fuel contract with the Reich which secured the future of the project and looked to be highly profitable. I.G. Farben and the Third Reich were now linked, and Hitler had been given the means to pursue a major war.

In 1935, Carl Duisberg died. He had been in effective control of BASF and then I.G. Farben since before the Great War. His protégé Carl Bosch had followed him as chair of the board of I.G. Farben and now he stepped up to take over as Chair of the supervisory board. His successor as chair of the board, Hermann Schmitz, was also from BASF; a national socialist sympathiser who would have no hesitation in allowing the company to co-operate with the regime in its preparations for war. By 1934/1935, I.G. Farben was setting up the structures which would allow it to liaise closely with the national socialist regime. Directed by Krauch, also a board member, a Vermittlungsstelle Wehrmacht or military liaison office was set up and staffed within I.G. Farben which, although later denied by the participants, was designed to prepare for a future war.

The period 1936 to 1939 was hugely successful and profitable for I.G. Farben and its constituent companies.

In the defining act of co-operation and which was to lead to trials in Nuremberg, I.G. Farben was to build two new factories, one in the east, safe from allied bombs. On behalf of the I.G., Otto Ambros sought out suitable locations in occupied Silesia and finally decided on one at what was then a small town called Auschwitz. Among its many advantages was the fact that there was already a concentration camp with 7000 inmates to provide construction slave labour in co-operation with the SS (who were, of course, paid for the slave labour they supplied; the enterprise was after all a capitalist undertaking). The Auschwitz area was completely agricultural. That meant the people of the area knew little of industrial work, and trained workers would have to be brought in to work on the plant. The intention was to build one of the largest factories in the world complete with housing, schools, and all the requirements of a large company town.

The population of the town of Auschwitz was made up of 4000 Jews, 7000 Poles, and 2000 German peasants. The SS was to expel the Jews and Poles from the area and put them into concentration camps. Their homes would serve as suitable quarters to accommodate construction workers and later on factory staff. (Yavner, 1984)

The horrors of Auschwitz and its adjacent camp Birkenau will not be repeated here. What is often little appreciated is that four miles from the main concentration camp, I.G. Farben and its constituent companies were constructing a huge factory using slave labour, with thousands of their employees (sometimes along with their families) from the company's plants in Germany engaged in the enterprise. The idea that the terrible activities at Auschwitz were in some remote Silesian forest and could not have been known of in Germany is nonsense; exchanges of personnel and information within one of the world's largest companies was taking place constantly and would certainly have been documented in detail, as is usual within major German public companies.

"Himmler preferred Auschwitz to the other Polish death camps because of the fraudulent status it had acquired through the plans to build the buna plant. The Jews could be sent east thinking they were going to work on the plant without suspecting the real purpose of their trip. Therefore, Auschwitz had the double task of providing forced labour for I.G. Farben while serving as a center for the mass extermination of the Jews." (Yavner)

Several members of the I.G. board visited Auschwitz between 1942 and 1944, some many times. Because of the distance from the main camp, I.G. Farben set up its own concentration camp, Monowitz, nearer to the building site of the new factory, where I.G. Farben assumed responsibility for the housing, feeding and health of the inmates, while the SS remained in charge of the security, punishment, and supply of inmates. According to Yavner, Gustav Herzog, an inmate whose responsibility it was to draw up the death lists in Monowitz, estimated that 120,000 inmate deaths could be traced to I.G. Auschwitz and Monowitz.

Auschwitz/Birkenau turned into a large company town with a constant and large-scale exchange of personnel at all levels within the companies concerned; mainly BASF and Bayer.

After the fall of Nazi Germany, the Allies began a process of de-Nazification, concentrating on what they considered to be the main perpetrators of the many crimes committed. There was, however, a distinct disinclination to look for and pursue senior members of the business community who may have had a connection to those crimes. There was a great interest on the part of both the US and British authorities in obtaining commercial secrets and key technical personnel but little appetite to bring senior businessmen to justice, should that prove necessary. This was particularly true of the British, who seemed convinced that German businesspeople must be innocent of any wrongdoing and should just get on with rebuilding Germany. Despite a general unwillingness of the US authorities to investigate business involvement with the Nazis, one Nuremberg prosecutor, Brigadier General Telford Taylor and his team pursued the available evidence and against resistance finally managed to bring cases against a number of I.G. Farben board members and senior employees. Krauch, chairman of the Aufsichtsrat, Schmitz, chairman of the Vorstand, and all the Vorstand members, were indicted, along with a number of senior managers, but the case was severely hampered by the fact that, shortly before and after the end of the war, large-scale destruction of important papers and documents took place throughout the I.G. Farben companies, leaving little evidence of the activities of those involved. However, enough survived to enable the prosecution, together with witness testimony, to make a case against the accused.

Despite what the prosecution considered overwhelming evidence, only eight of the defendants were found guilty of any crime. Although indicted on five different charges, the eight defendants were found guilty on two only: imprisonment and mass murder, and spoliation and plunder. The defence of Carl Krauch used an argument likely to resonate with US judges: "Replace IG by ICI for England [sic], or Dupont for America, or Montecatini for Italy and at once the similarity will become clear to you." In other words, Carl Krauch was simply an honest, industrious, God-fearing businessman who had worked for his country's defence – just as any patriotic American would have done on behalf of the United States. (Jeffreys)

The fear of communism and the need to rebuild industrial Germany as a bulwark led to a notable difference in the treatment of senior industrialists and other accused.

Whilst cases were brought against Krupp and Flick, the emphasis here is on I.G. Farben, and the role its management played. Whilst initially anxious to prosecute industrialists, this intent waned when subjected to criticism from United States industrialists and business, and the desire to fight the communist menace took precedence.

It is instructive to link together the sentences of the accused (in fact they served only a small part of the sentences, all being released early) and their later careers. Otto Ambros and Walter Duerrfeld both received eight years for slavery and mass murder. Ambros went on to become either chair or a member of the board of Chemie Gruenental, Pintsch Bmag AG, Knoll AG, Telefunken GmbH, Berliner Handelsgesellschaft and numerous other businesses, as well as a consultant to a US firm.

Fritz ter Meer, Heinrich Buetefisch, and Carl Krauch received seven, six, and six years' imprisonment respectively. ter Meer was elected to the board of Bayer AG and in 1955 became its chairman, as well as being chairman, deputy chairman or a board member of a number of other large companies. Buetefisch became a board member of Ruhr-Chemie and other companies, and Krauch joined the board of Huels, a successor company to I.G. Farben.

Georg von Schnitzler, Hermann Schmitz and Max Ilgner received five, four, and three years' imprisonment respectively. Schnitzler, who was the only person involved who appreciated the enormity of what had occurred, stayed out of business life. Schmitz, in contrast, joined the board of a major bank, Berlin West, and became chair of Rhein Steel. Max Ilgner took up religion.

Five other board members received two years' or eighteen months' imprisonment.

Today, and throughout the history of post-war Germany, Bayer and BASF have remained some of the biggest and most successful companies in the world. This success has been maintained over a period of 150 years, under a variety of democratic governments and non-democratic regimes. What myths are destroyed by this history, and what can we learn that may aid in understanding the underlying legal and political thinking in western Europe and the United States towards the limited company, and in undermining the supposed logic in that thinking?

The first exploded myth is that limited companies have an existence in themselves beyond the individual people running them. For this to be true, we would have to have experienced the sight of a copy of the legal foundation documents of Bayer and BASF, suitably framed, propped up on a chair in a Nuremberg courtroom and indicted with war crimes. Even this 'reductio ad absurdum' argument is too absurd. Only people can affect events and only people are responsible for their actions through the medium of a company.

The second exploded myth is that limited companies or corporations are necessary to ensure or maintain democracy. The legal fiction of Bayer and BASF as Aktiengesellchaften existed and functioned efficiently and successfully under an absolute monarchy, a democratic republic, a fascist dictatorship, and another democratic republic, often with the same people in charge in the variety of political circumstances.

The third exploded myth is that limited companies or corporations are a force for good in society. Depending on the people who manage and run them, they are a neutral 'blank canvas', and have the potential to be useful organs of economic control, or dangerous organs of oppression and evil. They can only be controlled through the people who control them being aware of sanctions, carrying the full weight of the law, for acting illegally or, in an international law sense, immorally. This negates the fiction of the corporate veil and opens company management to civil control and sanctions where necessary.

It could be argued that this period in history is too extreme to justify making judgements about the nature of the limited company. This would be naive. It makes it easy because the choices made, and results, are so clear. It would be equally possible to delve into the histories of British companies during the height of the British Empire or US companies during periods before and after the occurrence of 'regime change' in various parts of the world to illustrate the inescapable fact that, although the accepted view is that companies only interact with the general public, their key and constant interaction is with the state, usually without the knowledge of its citizens.

This terrible period in European and world history gave rise to one of the most laudable developments of the later 20th century, the moves to delineate and protect human rights. This leads inevitably to the question: can limited liability companies have human rights and should they, themselves, be subject to human rights law?

Chapter 9
Human Rights and the Company

The fact that German industrial companies during the First World War encouraged, if not initiated, the use of deported slave labour from conquered countries, and in the Second World War used slave labour and built their own concentration camps in a financial relationship with the SS, shows that companies can commit breaches of human rights.

To be both exact and consistent, a company cannot breach the human rights of an individual; it does not have the capacity to do so. Only another individual can do that, using the name and assets of the company. In the case of severe breaches of human rights, it proved and should prove necessary to pierce the corporate veil, but at present it is necessary only to look at the question of whether a company and those running it should be subject to human rights laws, both in respect of applying those rights to others, and in itself being protected by human rights law.

First, however, we should briefly review the history and content of human rights law post-1945. Following the horrors of the Second World War, the United Nations Charter was signed on June 26th 1945 and included amongst its stated objectives "promoting and encouraging respect for human rights and for fundamental freedoms for all without distinction as to race, sex, language, or religion", but did not elaborate further on what constituted human rights. Following the setting up of the Commission, three major international human rights instruments: the Universal Declaration of Human Rights (adopted in 1948), the International Covenant on Civil and Political Rights (ICCPR) and the International Covenant on Economic, Social and Cultural Rights (ICESCR) (both adopted in 1966) were issued. As always, it is advisable to examine the original documents; in this case the Universal Declaration of Human Rights, adopted on December 10th 1948 and which, although only a declaration and without binding force, has subsequently come to be recognised as a universal yardstick of State conduct.

The wording of the Declaration is both magnificent and clear.

Article 1
All human beings are born free and equal in dignity and rights. They are endowed with reason and conscience and should act towards one another in a spirit of brotherhood.

It is concerned with, as you would expect, the human rights of human beings and this is quite clear from the wording of the rights to be protected; they could not in any event apply to companies. As we will see from other, later, human rights declarations, the only deviation from this clear emphasis on the individual is in respect of property rights.

Article 17
Everyone has the right to own property alone as well as in association with others.
No one shall be arbitrarily deprived of his property.

Here 'everyone' is more broadly drawn than every human being, as if the drafters are afraid of limiting the ownership of property to individuals. Aside from this one exception, the human rights referred to in the Universal Declaration are exactly that: the rights of individual human beings.

The United Nations Charter and the Universal Declaration of Human Rights led to the development of human rights bodies on three continents: Europe, the Americas, and Africa. The Organization of American States

(OAS) was founded in 1948 to promote regional peace, security, and development. A dual model is in place in the Americas, consisting of the Inter-American Commission, based in Washington D.C., and the Inter-American Court of Human Rights, based in San José, Costa Rica. Again, it is worth referring to the original declaration to identify the intent of the drafters and here the intention is clear.

AMERICAN CONVENTION ON HUMAN RIGHTS "PACT OF SAN JOSE, COSTA RICA" (B-32)
Article 1. Obligation to Respect Rights

2. For the purposes of this Convention, "person" means every human being.

After some recent institutional reforms, the African system now resembles the Inter-American system. The declaration is also clear on who it is intended to protect but once again the drafters have potentially broadened the scope in respect of property.

The African Charter on Human and Peoples' Rights
Article 2
Every individual shall be entitled to the rights and freedoms recognized and guaranteed in the present charter....

Article 14
The right of property shall be guaranteed. It may only be encroached upon in the interest of public need or in the general interest of the community and in accordance with the provisions of appropriate laws.

Of the three continents, the most advanced guarantee of human rights is to be found in Europe. The Statute of the Council of Europe was signed in London on May 5th 1949, setting up the Council of Europe. There are presently forty-seven member states, and the organisation is separate from the European Union. The European Convention on Human Rights was signed on November 4th 1950 and as well as including in Section II the intent to set up a European Court of Human Rights, included as one of its aims:

Being resolved, as the governments of European countries which are like-minded and have a common heritage of political traditions, ideals, freedom and the rule of law, to take the first steps for the collective enforcement of certain of the rights stated in the Universal Declaration.

These rights were the rights of individual human beings and were, by definition, incapable of being applied to companies, as is clear from the list:

- **the right to life (Article 2)**
- **freedom from torture (Article 3)**
- **freedom from slavery (Article 4)**
- **the right to liberty (Article 5)**
- **the right to a fair trial (Article 6)**
- **the right not to be punished for something that wasn't against the law at the time (Article 7)**
- **the right to respect for family and private life (Article 8)**
- **freedom of thought, conscience and religion (Article 9)**
- **freedom of expression (Article 10)**
- **freedom of assembly (Article 11)**
- **the right to marry and start a family (Article 12)**
- **the right not to be discriminated against in respect of these rights (Article 14)**

Later protocols added rights to the above list but in only one case, to be expected; that of property rights, deviated from the clear intent to encompass only human beings in the declaration.

- **the right to protection of property (Protocol 1, Article 1)**
- **the right to education (Protocol 1, Article 2)**
- **the right to participate in free elections (Protocol 1, Article 3)**
- **the abolition of the death penalty (Protocol 13)**

Protocol 1, Article 1 from 1952 is clear in including 'legal persons' under property rights although the article is formulated so as not to limit the powers of the state to make any laws considered necessary to 'control the use of property'.

Every natural or legal person is entitled to the peaceful enjoyment of his possessions. No one shall be deprived of his possessions except in the public interest and subject to the conditions provided for by law and by the general principles of international law.

The preceding provisions shall not, however, in any way impair the right of a State to enforce such laws as it deems necessary to control the use of property in accordance with the general interest or to secure the payment of taxes or other contributions or penalties.

Nowhere in either the original Universal Declaration of Human Rights or in any of the subsequent regional declarations is there evidence of any intent that they should also include limited liability, or indeed any, companies under the declaration, except for one clear use of language in the European Declaration of Human Rights in respect of property. The European Court of Human Rights sees this differently and has accepted cases by companies on a case-by-case basis, assessing whether there is room for using certain articles of the Convention regarding companies, although these are mainly related to the protection of property, especially in cases of nationalisation of real estate or changes in regulations governing land use.

"The inclusion of 'legal persons' in Protocol 1 has had a significant impact on the concept of rights in Europe and proved to be a watershed for the endorsement of the principle that corporations can be entitled to human rights protections.

"But corporations cannot be held accountable for human rights violations. So, while corporations can be protected by human rights law, they can at the same time enjoy impunity for committing human rights violations... of 3,307 judgments delivered in the European Court of Human Rights between 1998-2003, 126 (or 3.8%) originated in applications filed by companies or other persons pursuing corporate interests."[47]

Although as a member of the Council of Europe the United Kingdom was a signatory to the European Convention on Human Rights and recognised the European Court of Human Rights, in 1998 the Human Rights Act set out the fundamental rights and freedoms that everyone in the UK is entitled to under the Convention. It incorporates the rights set out in the European Convention on Human Rights into domestic British law. The Human Rights Act came into force in the UK in October 2000. This meant that it became possible to take a case to a British court rather than to the

---

[47] How human rights law has been used to guarantee corporations a 'right to profit'. Published: March 17, 2017, David Whyte and Dr Stephanie Khoury

European Court of Human Rights. Despite leaving the European Union, the United Kingdom remains a signatory to the European Convention on Human Rights.

It is reasonable and necessary that any new companies act should specifically exclude limited and other companies from protection under the human rights acts.

The question as to whether companies should be subject to human rights law has already been answered with a resounding yes. It is only necessary to fill in the details.

The human rights laws promulgated after the Second World War were the direct product of atrocities committed by states and companies as a review of the rights to be protected shows; Articles 2, 3, 4 and 5 were aimed as much at corporate crimes as at state crimes. Had Telford Taylor been prosecuting German industrialists and senior managers in the 1950s, he would only have had to supply the plentiful evidence of breaches of human rights law for the defendants to have been found guilty. The judges would simply have had to apply existing law and not have to create law as they did in Nuremberg in 1947, where Taylor was putting forward charges which had previously not been recognised. They would, therefore, have been unable to exculpate the defendants of many crimes as they appeared to do. The crimes were committed under the legal cover of I.G. Farben, using that company's assets and personnel; it should not be forgotten that in the 1930s and 1940s I.G. Farben had the size and outreach of many smaller European countries.

Failing to make companies subject to human rights law is to ignore this power available to the leaders of these companies, which can make them as influential and powerful as many state politicians. Although crimes are committed in the name of, and under the protection of, companies, once they have been identified and prosecuted, the corporate veil must at once be lifted and directors and senior managers prosecuted under human rights law as they were in Nuremberg.

A recent United Nations report drew attention to the law related to companies by including the following passages;

III. Legal context

12. Today, some corporate conglomerates exceed the gross domestic product (GDP) of entire sovereign States.   ... Sometimes wielding more power – political, economic and discursive – than States themselves, corporations enjoy increasing recognition as rights holders, with still insufficient corresponding obligations. The asymmetry of immense power without sufficiently justiciable accountability exposes a fundamental global governance gap.

14. Nevertheless, important precedents exist. The post-Holocaust industrialists' trials, such as the I.G. Farben trial, laid the groundwork for recognizing the international criminal responsibility of corporate executives for participation in international crimes.

16. Today, the Guiding Principles on Business and Human Rights set out the normative framework for States' and corporate entities' compliance with international law. States have the primary obligation to prevent, investigate, punish and remedy human rights abuses by third parties, and may breach their obligations if they fail to do so. The Guiding Principles crystallize the human rights standards applicable to corporate conduct that apply regardless of whether States uphold their primary obligations. International humanitarian law and criminal law also confer specific obligations and liabilities on private actors, with domestic jurisdictions primarily responsible for enforcement.

17. The Guiding Principles establish a continuum of responsibilities, depending on whether corporate entities cause, contribute to or are directly linked with adverse human rights impacts. 24 In conflicts, businesses must observe heightened human rights due diligence to identify concerns and adjust their conduct. 25 The liability of corporate entities will be determined by their actions and by the human rights impact: due diligence is not sufficient to absolve corporations of liability. 26 At a minimum, corporate entities directly linked to human rights impacts must exercise leverage or consider termination of their activities or relationships. Failure to act accordingly may give rise to liability. Where violations constitute crimes, corporate executives and, increasingly, entities themselves, may be held accountable for their knowledge of and material contributions to crimes.

UN Human Rights Council
Fifty-ninth session
16 June–11 July 2025

Companies must be subject to all laws, which must include human rights law. Occurrences will be rare, as they are with state breaches (at present), but this argument is never used to suggest that human rights laws should be abandoned per se, and the power of these laws should be available to prosecute powerful companies in the future.

Nazi Germany controlled and used German companies for its purposes but was unable to force other countries to use or give special treatment to them. The 21st Century has seen countries use their economic and military power to support individual or groups of companies and use coercion against other independent states which adds yet another dimension to the need for countries to review their own laws. This was common in the colonial age but is new and frightening when used against other democratic countries. No one expected or predicted the atrocities of the 1930s and 1940s, and it is likely that no one will predict such inevitable future events.

Finding Solutions

Chapter 10
A 19th Century Approach in the 20th Century

A Legal View

We will see that statutory company law in the UK is limited and confines itself principally to matters of internal company regulation. Much of the law under which companies operate is, because of the United Kingdom's legal basis of common law, judge-made in a succession of legal cases. When important legal precedence is set in a series of cases there is cause for concern, as judges do not operate in a vacuum; they are the product of their background and of the legal mores prevalent during their formative years. The traditional view is that although the role of a judge is creative, it is not a legislative one. The judicial role is not one of making law, nor is it one of finding law; it is to make the law through a creative interpretation of existing legal resources.

For 19th century legal theorists and philosophers, this concept presented no challenge. For 20th century theorists, dangers inherent in this process in a democratic age could no longer be avoided. The legal systems of both the United Kingdom and the United States are based on common law, and it was mainly American lawyers who raised questions related to judge-made law. The problem of the role of the judge and the belief that it had been inadequately explained led to efforts by such theorists as Fuller, Pound and Dworkin to find a justification and explanation of judicial creativity.

If judges are creatures of their time and are basing judgements on earlier judicial decisions made similarly by judges also creatures of their time, is it not possible that legal outcomes reflect prior structures of political power, not current social or political values?

What is most interesting about the reflections of the earlier 20th century legal theorists is that a concept often selected for analysis and criticism is the problem of the nature of corporate personality.

H.L.A. Hart, in his Oxford inaugural lecture, uses this issue as "an illustration of the sterility of much conceptual analysis of legal philosophy... the legal meaning of 'corporation' can be understood only by considering linguistic contexts in which the concept is invoked. There is nothing which can be identified with what law treats as a corporation or as corporate personality."[48]

In an essay on legal realism (1935), Felix Cohen considers issues of corporate personality in this way. "Hence, instead of asking how particular social or economic goals are best to be served through a certain regulatory decision – for example, whether a trade union should be subject to liability in tort for the actions of its members – courts in Britain and the United States considered whether a trade union is a person in law, an issue which when phrased in abstract terms, is akin to the apocryphal scholastic dispute as to how many angels can stand on the point of a needle."[49]

The abstract question of personality is apparently treated as determining whether or not there can be liability. Legal theorists term this 'reification'. Legal ideas seem to take on a life of their own. Legal reasoning becomes a form of mystification; it is possible to theorise about the meaning of

---

[48] The Politics of Jurisprudence. R Cotterell (University of Pennsylvania Press, 1992).
[49] Ibid.

'corporate personality' without considering the policy and purpose which the concepts reflect.

It is important to record that there is extensive and informed criticism of the extra-statutory development of law regulating companies. Referencing the legal historian Morton Horwitz, Cotterell notes: "the particular concepts of corporate personality ... had special importance in legitimating the concentration of economic wealth and power in big business in the United States in the late 19th century. The 'natural entity' conception which saw the corporation not as a legal creature of the state or as the agent of its members but as an autonomous abstract entity in law made it possible, to justify freeing corporations from legal restraints, for example on their ability to own the stock of other corporations."[50]

I would add that this argument can be applied equally well to UK developments over an even longer period and, indeed, throughout the 20th century.

It was important, before setting out a structure for a radical new companies act, to emphasize the judge-made nature of much regulation of companies, and how it is of its period and has been the subject of review and criticism for most of the 20th century. This should be understood before taking a closer look at the current law in relation to companies, the act of 2006, and how, in the 21st century, it has reached its present form.

---

[50] Ibid.

1948 to 2004

With some very minor adjustments from the Companies Act 1967, the Companies Act 1948 was the law governing UK companies until it was changed for the first time because of outside influence.

On January 1st 1973 Britain joined the then European Economic Community (EEC) and over the following twenty years European Directives were issued, aimed at the limited harmonisation of company law throughout the EEC. This attempt at convergence was driven by the right of establishment protected by Article 49 (ex-Article 43) of the Treaty of Rome (this treaty has changed its name over time, originally signed in Rome in 1957 as the Treaty establishing the European Economic Community then becoming the Treaty establishing the European Community and finally the Treaty on the functioning of the European Union) and the speed, frequency and nature of changes to company law during this period are not comparable with the glacial nature of change over the preceding 100 years.

In a House of Lords debate, Lord Mais put the issue concisely:

"One of the major problems in the drafting of the company law Directives has been to reconcile the prescriptive and codified approach of the original six Member States with the more flexible and often non-statutory approach adopted by this country. The contrast between the British and the Continental system is that we in Britain rely to a considerable extent on the city institutions to regulate or to control, while the continental system relies a great deal on statutory regulations and rigid statutory control."[51]

The volume of changes to company law in the period 1973

---

[51] EEC Company Law Proposals HL Deb 08 April 1976 vol 369 cc1835-78.

up to the 2006 Companies Act is extensive but it is useful to have an overview of the major amendments arising from European Union Directives and Regulations in this period in order to identify and evaluate the changes they brought and to consider any implication which may arise now that the United Kingdom has left the European Union.

A second strand pushing changes in UK company law during this period was the perceived need for corporate law to be internationally competitive in the race to attract inward investment and multi-national companies to Britain. This belief was closely tied to the concept of globalisation.

There will be pressure to make changes to British company law now that we are no longer in the EU and changes may be necessary but not a reversion to the pre-1973 laissez-faire tradition or to the misconceived rush to accommodate 'globalised' companies.

The period 1980 to date presents a particular challenge. A large number of the many changes to company law were the result of EU directives and regulations, but did the changes they initiated result in a profound change to earlier principles, and did they change the nature of British company law? The short answer is no and, therefore, this area of change can best be dealt with separately from any changes initiated by the British Government in this period.

The European Union summarises the aims of harmonisation as follows:

"There is no codified European company law as such, and Member States continue to operate separate company acts, which are amended from time to time to comply with EU directives and regulations.

"Although there is no codified European company law as such, harmonisation of the national rules on company law has created some minimum standards."[52]

Again the main concern was with protecting shareholders, financial reporting and disclosure.

When considering the changes to company law initiated by the British Government in this period, two factors must be taken into account: firstly, there is a "deeply ingrained reliance on market-based regulatory solutions to company problems" and secondly, "the dominance of private sector business groups in Britain has meant that successive governments were reluctant to legislate in regard to the control of companies and accepted that self-regulatory and market-based solutions were more likely to be effective ways of restraining corporate abuses."[53] This was also the period during which the free-market economic theories identified with Professor Friedman and the 'Chicago School' achieved wide acceptance, particularly in the US and Britain, and ensured that any amendments to company law were likely to be free-market in nature.

EU company law directives represented a departure from the traditional approach to British law, as previously company law had not set out detailed requirements relating to the preparation of accounts, the valuation of assets and liabilities, and the calculation of profit and loss. Any standardisation had earlier been regulated through standards issued by professional bodies but now these matters had to be dealt with in the individual member states by legislation. In respect of individual companies, this was achieved in Britain by the 1981 Companies Act implementing the EU Fourth Directive and for group accounts by the 1989 Act implementing the EU Seventh Directive. In respect of group accounts, this was not such a

---

[52] European Parliament Fact Sheet

[53] Corporate Law Modernisation and Corporate Governance in the UK - some recent issues and debates. Professor Roman Tomasic.

material departure for Britain, as these had been a requirement of company law since 1947, and since the early 1940s the Stock Exchange had required newly listed companies to do this.

The effect of the Seventh Directive was to spread the net to include companies, unincorporated associations and partnerships which had previously been excluded from consolidation. The most far-reaching change was introduced into British company law following the implementation of the Second Directive; EU directives were targeted at larger companies and whilst Britain only had one class of company, many EU states differentiated between larger or public companies and private companies (for example, the German Aktiengesellschaft [AG], the public company, and the Gesellschaft mit beschrankter Haftung [GmbH], the private company). This led to the introduction of a new definition of 'public company' or PLC in Britain, with private companies forming a residual category of company. Following this change, the future differentiation between public and private companies was mainly in the direction of the deregulation of private companies.

2004 to Date

The Companies Act 2006 is said to be the largest piece of legislation ever passed by Parliament, with 1300 sections and sixteen schedules. By contrast, the 1948 Companies Act had 462 schedules, the 1985 Act 747, the 1989 Act an added 216 schedules. How different is the 2006 Act from the Acts of 1856, 1862 or 1948? Is UK company law intrinsically different from the past because of this mammoth act?

For a technical, as opposed to a political or economic, answer, it is best to turn to legal commentators. Around 400 additional clauses were introduced as the legislation passed through Parliament, however:

"The growth of the Act during its progress through Parliament was largely not the result of substantive new measures being added. Instead, it came about because of the restatement of existing provisions of the 1985, 1989 and 2004 Companies Acts"[54] and, "The Act is longer than the existing Companies Acts in part because the drive for simplification has led to a less concise, but easier to understand, drafting style."[55]

What were the substantive changes in the 2006 Companies Act which called for these 1300 sections?

"The Act is in many respects deregulatory – with private companies benefiting most – but there are also a number of areas where new obligations or potential burdens are introduced, particularly for publicly traded companies. The result is a widening gap between the regulatory burden for publicly traded companies and that for private companies, which could encourage many more businesses to stay or go private."[56]

The keywords are clear: no substantive new measures, but the continued deregulation of private companies.

The 2006 Act is in substance a 19th century document modestly updated in limited areas by the requirements of the European Union. Despite being an immense piece of legislation, it is overwhelmingly inward-looking and is concerned with the members (the owners) almost exclusively, although to a limited extent it is also concerned with the creditors of a company, but with little beyond these two groups.

---

[54] The ICSA Companies Act 2006 Handbook, 2nd Edition. Consultant Editor Keith Walmsley.
[55] Ibid.
[56] Ibid.

It is no longer possible to avoid considering some details of the Act, but this will be kept as brief as possible and is only intended to allow the interested reader to see the extremely limited extent to which sections of this huge Act are concerned with matters external to the company.

Sections 1060 to 1120 of the Act set up a Registrar of Companies which makes public the formation of a company in the Gazette or by other means. The Registrar of Companies files, which are open to public inspection, include the documents needed to set up the company, details of the directors, the accounts filed annually, reports and returns, and the address of the registered office of the company. Section 1078 (3) extends the requirements for public companies but again these are very much of concern to and for the owners of the company and are mainly concerned with share capital.

The most obvious area where the company is open to outside view, but not influence, is the requirement to present annual audited financial statements (sections 380 to 474). These allow the citizen and the state to assess the financial health of the company and to be assured that it is a 'going concern'; that is, is it unlikely to fail in the near future? From the point of view of the auditor tasked with confirming this, it means that the company is financially in a position to survive for the next accounting period, usually twelve months, and at least until the next annual audit. This is comforting but has no impact on the running of the company, and the rate of unpredicted collapse of major companies in recent years leaves limited confidence in the process.

The power to make external investigations into a company (sections 1035 to 1039) is solely in the hands of the Secretary of State, who has the power to appoint and to define the remit of inspectors. The brevity of this area of the act and the limited use made of it by governments shows how little importance need be attached to these powers.

Companies must report publicly political donations and expenses. The Act requires that these are authorised by a resolution of shareholders, but a single resolution can cover the holding company and one or more of its subsidiaries. This promotes visibility of political ties but suggests that these are acceptable and part and parcel of company activity.

The sections of the Act which one would expect to take an external view and show an element of responsibility to the citizen and the state beyond that to the owners (shareholders) are those relating to directors and their responsibilities. A company has no physical existence other than a registration certificate and a bundle of other documents. Every action of a company, large or small, must be carried out by human agents, and at the top of the pinnacle of human agents are the company's directors.

One would expect an act drafted in the 21st century to make some demands on the directors to, at the very least, not cause damage to citizens or state, but this was not the case. For the first time, the Act codified directors' duties, but this has to be treated with caution as it is not comprehensive and although it introduced the concept of "enlightened shareholder value" or principles of corporate social responsibility, it was unclear to what extent, if any, the Act created new and onerous duties, or whether it simply reflected what companies were already doing. Again, most of the seven duties of directors relate to their responsibilities to the owners (shareholders); only one relates to external actors.

The duties set out in the Act are:

1. To act within powers, directors must act in accordance with the company's constitution.

2. To promote the success of the company. The concept of 'enlightened shareholder value' [the clue is in the name] is included in this section and amongst other matters requires the directors to have regard to:

> • The likely consequences of any decision in the long-term.
>
> •The interests of the company's employees.
>
> •The need to foster the company's business relationships with suppliers, customers and others.
>
> •The impact of the company's operations on the community and the environment.
>
> •The desirability of the company maintaining a reputation for high standards of business conduct.
>
> •The need to act as between members of the company.

3. To exercise independent judgement.

4. To exercise reasonable care, skill and diligence.

5. To avoid conflicts of interest.

6. Not to accept benefits from third parties.

7. To declare interests in proposed transactions with the company.

Have sections 170 to 181 changed or extended the duties a director may have to anyone other than the owners contained in earlier Companies Acts? Informed legal opinion is that they have not, and nor were they intended to; the wording is deliberately vague and there are no penalties for any breach. This a fine example of 'nullum crimen sine lege'; there is no offence without a law, and this law was deliberately imprecise.

In the House of Lords, the Attorney-General, Lord Goldsmith, said: "There is nothing in the Bill that says there is a need for a paper trail... I do not agree that the effect of passing this Bill will be that directors will be subject to a breach if they cannot demonstrate that they have considered every element. It will be for the person who is asserting breach of duty to make the case good."

So, after 170 years of company law, as clearly said in Parliament, whilst directors should "have regard to the various factors stated, that requirement is subordinate to the overriding duty to promote the success of the company."[57]

[57] Margaret Hodge, Hansard col 591, 11th July 2006.

Chapter 11
A Principled Approach

The overriding question when considering a new company law is: is the limited liability company (company) necessary?

The response must be an unequivocal yes, the scale of industry and commercial activity in the 21st century being such that if the limited liability company did not exist, one would have to legislate for something similar.

If we were, however, now creating the company on a blank sheet of paper, what would we wish to create that would meet the economic and commercial requirements of the 21st century and the legitimate expectations of the citizens of a democracy?

Company law in the UK dates substantially from the mid-19th century. How should one approach the task of reviewing it and proposing an alternative for the 21st century? As we have seen, the Companies Act 2006 is substantially a 19th century document amended by the requirements of the European Union. The interface of a company via company law with society, its employees and country or region is minimal, which mattered little in the 19th century when company law developed. Companies were incorporated for specific purposes, were usually highly capitalised, were confined generally to Great Britain, and were not part of a worldwide web of interrelated companies. This changed markedly throughout the 20th century, but the law remained unchanged. How should we envisage a companies act for the 21st century, in view of all the other changes which have occurred over the last 170 years? Representative democracy, human rights law, environmental laws and interests, health and safety laws and concerns and, just as importantly, the power available via technology to gather and use vast quantities of information about citizens, amongst other things.

This is such an obvious point that it is worth expanding on it to cover the large so-called tech companies. As new technologies appear, companies use them, a typical example being the long-standing production of cars and other vehicles. These companies are not, however, allowed to produce whatever they wish: factors such as safety and emissions-control circumscribe their activities and what they can produce and sell. It would be unthinkable for a car-producing company to insist on producing a dangerous and high-emission vehicle on the principle that government should not interfere in the market or with company activity.

Companies must follow the laws of the country in which they operate and because the 'tech' companies wish to market a product unrestrained by law or regulation for the world, individual countries believe this presents them with a problem. The correct view is that using this model presents the companies concerned with a problem.

For political reasons (usually financial) in the United States, the owners of companies are often conflated with the company and Zuckerberg and Bezos et al explaining what they will and will not do blurs the issue, probably deliberately. But the necessary protection of the citizen, together with the need to collect taxes, justifies a simple change in the law and for the companies involved to follow it. The economic power of the European Union proves the advantage of countries grouping together to ensure that failure to follow law and regulation imposes sufficient pressure on large companies for them to comply.

Serious reviews have not taken place because of the perceived complexity and benign nature of the law, so that any review needs a framework to make the process clear and transparent and to give structure to the process. It would also help to place the review in the framework of political philosophy.

The overarching political philosophy of the 19th century (and earlier) was utilitarianism. Identified with Hume, Adam Smith, Bentham and John Stuart Mill, this philosophy defined the United Kingdom of the 19th and 20th centuries and pervaded its legislation. "The great utilitarians... were social theorists and economists of the first rank; and the moral doctrine they worked out was framed to meet the needs of their wider interests and to fit into a comprehensive scheme."[58]

In utilitarian theory, "a society is properly arranged when its institutions maximise the net balance of satisfaction. The principle of choice for an association of men is interpreted as an extension of the principle of choice for one man."[59]

"It does not matter, except indirectly, how this sum of satisfactions is distributed among individuals any more than it matters, except indirectly, how one man distributes his satisfactions over time. The correct distribution in either case is that which yields the maximum fulfilment."[60]

The problem with this view is clear; as justice has not got priority over satisfaction, nothing prevents utilitarian theory accepting not only gross inequality but also injustice. Taken to an extreme, it could justify the enslaving or subjugating of a minority for the benefit (satisfaction) of the majority.

In Bentham's own words: "An action then may be said to be conformable to the principle of utility, or, for shortness sake, to utility (meaning with respect to the community at large), when the tendency it has to augment the happiness

---

[58] A Theory of Justice, John Rawls, Harvard, 1971.
[59] Ibid.
[60] Ibid.

of the community is greater than any it has to diminish it."[61]

Given that utilitarian political theory lies at the root of 19th century legislation, a new review is best made from the standpoint of a different theory, updated and redirected to enable it to be used as an analytical tool.

In A Theory of Justice, John Rawls renewed and redefined contract theory and, by placing justice at the core of his theory, he drew a firm line between utilitarianism and contract theory and supplied a framework which makes possible a critical analysis of company law in the 21st century. Rawls' book is concerned with moral philosophy and with justice in society and, whilst being also concerned with institutions, it will be necessary to justify applying its principles to the company. This is particularly so as a defence of the company today would almost certainly be made based on utilitarian principles. A short overview is set out below, but a more extensive explanation and justification for borrowing Rawls' theories is needed and is set out later in this chapter.

In Part I, Chapter I, The Role of Justice, Rawls sets out his principles.

"These principles are the principles of social justice: they provide a way of assigning rights and duties in the basic institutions of society, and they define the appropriate distribution of the benefits and burdens of social co-operation."

The key words here are 'the basic institutions of society'. I have no doubt that Rawls intended to refer to the great offices of state and national institutions, but the world has changed quite fundamentally in the last fifty years and for the citizens of the United Kingdom, and to a great extent those of the wider world, the dominant institution today is

---

[61] Jeremy Bentham, 1780, An Introduction to the Principles of Morals and Legislation. Chapter 1.

the limited liability company in it various forms. There are now around 4.5 million companies in the United Kingdom, and it is impossible for the adult citizen to avoid contact of some sort with them many times each day. As well as choosing to buy from a company, most citizens will be employed by one (or more) and will have optional and non-optional public services provided by one or more companies. Companies have largely taken over functions which formerly were believed to be the function of the state, and there is no indication that this process is slowing down.

It is impossible to talk about the basic institutions of society without including the company. Rawls defines an institution as follows:

"Now by an institution I shall understand a public system of rules which defines offices and positions with their rights and duties, powers and immunities, and the like. These rules specify certain forms of action are permissible and others forbidden, and they provide for certain penalties and defences, and so on, when violations occur... An institution exists at a certain time and place when the actions specified by it are regularly carried out in accordance with a public understanding that the system of rules defining the institution is to be followed."

In his first chapter, part two, on the 'Subject of Justice', Rawls provides a justification for including his theory in a review of the company as he includes 'private property in the means of production' as a subject, which must include the limited liability company as the most prolific worldwide structure devoted to private property in the means of production. Rawls' work is complex and erudite, but it is necessary to give a brief overview of how it will be used in the later chapters as a basis of analysis.

Despite being based on contract theory, there is no intent to postulate an initial contract; rather to set out the principles of justice for the basic structure of society. These are the principles that "free and rational persons concerned to further their own interests would accept in an initial position of equality as defining the fundamental terms of their association... These principles are to regulate all further agreements; they specify the kinds of social cooperation that can be entered into and the forms of government that can be established."[62]

Before touching on the principles underlying the theory, a particularly valuable theoretical concept used by Rawls must be emphasised. In applying the principles of justice to what Rawls terms 'the original position', the parties do not know certain facts:

- No-one knows their place in society, their class position, or how they are endowed with natural assets and abilities such as intelligence and strength.
- Equally, they are unaware of how their life will progress or their psychological makeup, such as aversion to risk. In this state, parties also know little about their society, other than their general understanding of the principles of justice.
- Finally, they are also not aware of which generation they belong to so that any chosen principles must be fair inter-generationally.

These factors form what Rawls terms the 'veil of ignorance', which I will use in later analysis.

The important consequence of this concept is that parties have no basis for bargaining and therefore no-one is able to use principles for their own advantage. Equally, banding together in groups would present no advantage as no

---

[62] A Theory of Justice, John Rawls, Harvard, 1971.

individual can identify themselves or their advantage. This is the position as set out for a theoretical first negotiation but, as Rawls showed, his theories can be used also to investigate individual institutions and, though not spelled out directly, should be capable of minor amendment to apply them to a more limited current application.

It is therefore reasonable to propose that in reviewing the 21st century company law, those parties conducting the review should be unaware of their position in society; their natural abilities; even their generation. It is also reasonable to assume that the parties are aware of current political structures and, more importantly, the fact that equality and justice are basically entrenched in their society (the Human Rights Act, European Court of Human Rights) together with a sound judicial system.

Veil of Ignorance

A person choosing principles of justice must be ignorant of factors that would lead them to favour their own interests. As noted above, a person behind such a veil of ignorance is in an original position, and we postulate which principles of justice they would choose. By extension, this principle can be extended to the choices to be made by our persons behind the veil of ignorance (in respect of personal knowledge) regarding the legal rules and regulation to be included in a new company law (the blank sheet of paper).

In outlining future amendments and additions to company law, we will consider whether this 'informed citizen' would agree to the changes, and why.

Using this approach in respect of the interaction of a company with society, the citizen and the government is relatively straightforward. More challenging is its application to the situation of the employee of a company. In theory, the position is uncomplicated; the employee has a contractual relationship with the company. What this means in practice is less clear because of the disparity of power between the employee and the company, particularly when the company is large. This power imbalance can be mitigated to some extent by the existence of and membership in a trade union. However, the law regulating trade unions is subject to amendment and limitation. In the interest of justice, the right to belong to a trade union should be written into company law because Britain has now left the European Union and pressure may increase to reverse many of the employee legal protections provided by that membership.

More on the Theory of Justice

One key question when discussing the future of the company is the relevance of justice as a concept. 'Justice' is not a word often used in UK political discussion; we tend to use 'fairness' as an alternative. Being fair typically involves treating everyone the same or providing equal opportunities, while being just means giving individuals what they deserve based on their actions, needs, or circumstances, even if it means differential treatment.

Rawls presented a philosophical account of distributive justice which held a profound vision of the just society. Although he was concerned with the principles of justice, he was also clear that the concept of the original position and veil of ignorance could be applied to sections and other constructs of society. The need to apply this concept to the company arises from the dominant position which this legal construct has taken in modern society worldwide, and the extent to which it permeates society.

After centuries of utilitarianism being the dominant theory of political economy in Britain, a change of direction is particularly challenging, especially when being applied to an institution which is not usually considered to be subject to any theory. It is necessary, therefore, to set out briefly how contract theory as propounded by Rawls differs from traditional utilitarian theory (an important addition to the premise that the company requires social and political control) and the impact this might have on the nature of a company and to emphasise where utilitarianism differs from Rawls' contract theory.

"Each person possesses an inviolability founded on justice that even the welfare of society as a whole cannot override. For this reason, justice denies that the loss of freedom for some is made right by a greater good shared by others. It does not allow that the sacrifices imposed on a few are outweighed by the larger sum of advantages enjoyed by the many. Therefore, in a just society the liberties of equal citizenship are taken as settled; the rights secured by justice are not subject to political bargaining or to the calculus of social interests."[63]

These sentences summarise completely the difference between utilitarianism and contract theory, this statement could not exist under utilitarian principles.

"Political economy is importantly concerned with the public sector and the proper form of the background institutions that regulate economic activity, with taxation and the rights of property, the structure of markets, and so on."[64]

This sentence should indicate that repurposing Rawls' theories to encompass the company is justified and would meet with his approval.

---

[63] A Theory of Justice, John Rawls, Harvard, 1971.
[64] Ibid.

Chapter 12
The Next Steps

The company exists as a legal construct. It can be beneficial and if it did not exist it would have to be invented. Having said this, all aspects of it are open to review and revision. It has little to do with the 'market' and in a representative democracy it is a facilitating courtesy from the citizens, through their government, to enable large-scale business undertakings to be financed and managed. Its permitted structure and the controls over it are matters for the state, on behalf of its citizens and, provided those limitations are common to all, i.e. not discriminatory, they are legitimate. Language is important in this context; anyone can take part in the market through a variety of legal forms. If they choose to use a company, they are constrained by the current laws surrounding that form.

To be decided is what should be included in a new Companies Act. Any act should be as widely drawn as possible but there are aspects of legal responsibilities of companies which are difficult to include in detail in an act. Detailed taxation regulations and employment law, along with environmental law, spring to mind. The challenge is to ensure that companies follow these laws even if only by requiring companies to comply with all relevant laws. How this is to be enforced remains to be defined.

Some help can be given by reference to human rights law. Whilst difficult to define, human rights are assumed to have three inherent qualities, that they cannot be eroded by time (imprescriptible), they cannot be removed or relinquished (inalienable), and they cannot be overridden or superseded (indefeasible).

Under the European Convention on Human Rights, "Every natural person is entitled to the peaceful enjoyment of his possessions. No one shall be deprived of his possessions except in the public interest and subject to the conditions provided for by law and by the general principles of international law. The preceding provisions shall not, however, in any way impact the right of a state to enforce such laws as it deems necessary to control the use of property in accordance with the general interest or to secure the payment of taxes or other contributions or penalties."[65]

The term 'natural person' would exclude the artificial construct of a company. As a shareholder, you have a financial interest in the capital and residual value of the company, but no control over its assets. This is quite clear in the case of a large public company but is often overlooked in the case of a company owned by one individual.

The challenge will be to try to identify similar qualities relevant to company law which should be included in the new law.

When considering what controls and regulations to implement in respect of companies, a blank sheet of paper is the intended starting point. However, it would be unwise to ignore the huge amount of expert work by the United Kingdom government on risk reduction in relation to limited companies, in this case banks, following the 2008 financial crash. This financial catastrophe (not too strong a word for it) was the result of a total failure by a large section of the management of global financial institutions (companies) either to understand the nature of the risks they were taking, or to have understood yet deliberately ignored them. In any event, it was a management and system failure of

---

[65] European Convention on Human Rights, Article 1 of Protocol 1, The Right to Peaceful Enjoyment of Property.

immense consequence. Only by injecting vast quantities of their citizens' money were countries able to avoid the total collapse of the international financial structure.

Britain was severely affected as a result of having a financial sector that was large in relation to the rest of the economy. Having spent immense sums of citizens' money on rescuing the financial system, two results followed.

Firstly, government decided that, having at great cost allowed the citizens to bail out the banks and financial institutions, it was necessary to rapidly and continually recover the government financial position by severely cutting all aspects of social spending. Health, infrastructure, education, justice and the police, amongst others, were all subject to savage reductions in funding.

Secondly, government – slowly and belatedly – took steps to reduce the risk of a recurrence of the failure by introducing more stringent controls on bank and financial company boards' management and structures. It is useful to illustrate what controls and regulations government believed it necessary to aspire to (but not to legislate for) and to propose that these should be extended to cover all large companies in a redrawn companies act.

"Effective governance arrangements: the right tone from the top and a culture of risk awareness are key for the long-term success of the business. It all starts with a strong and well-functioning board, which sets the business strategy and risk appetite and provides effective leadership. Boards should have appropriate composition, balance, independence as well as knowledge, skills and experience. Boards should have appropriate conflicts of interest management procedures, adequate MI (Management Information) and appropriate succession plans. Effective governance arrangements ensure that all areas of the firm are well controlled and are subject to the appropriate oversight and independent challenge. It all starts with the board – a strong and well-functioning board is central to good governance – and this in turn requires a strong board chair."[66]

We are now in a position to establish the points of principle which should underpin a new company law, the reasons for choosing these, and the underlying justification.

---

[66] Bank of England Regulatory Expectations 2022, Bank of England.

Chapter 13
Points of Principle

In the context of 21st century Britain the aim is to draft a new outline of company law to which all informed citizens could agree in principle without knowing their position in society, whether monarch or rough sleeper. The state already has an advanced infrastructure of laws which must be followed by all citizens; ignorance of the law is no defence.

The overall goal is creation of a democratic state by and for the benefit of all its citizens.

This chapter will outline the eight highest points of principle before expanding into detail.

1. All companies are subject to all relevant laws.
2. Legal responsibility extends to the Board of Management and senior management.
3. Interaction between the company and the state must be transparent.
4. There is an absolute prohibition on company involvement in politics.
5. Large, economically important companies and companies supplying socially necessary services will be subject to added control and scrutiny.
6. All companies must be, and remain, adequately capitalised.
7. All companies must pay a fair and proportionate amount of tax.
8. Limited liability does not extend to subsidiary companies.

First Principle
All companies are subject to all relevant laws

The company, in respect of all its activities, must obey the law of the land. This is an apparently simple point which presents major challenges only if one accepts the traditional legal interpretation of the company.

How is this principle to be enforced? The present position, from an American perspective, is set out by Professor Greenfield in The Failure of Corporate Law:

"Most constructarians argue that the solution should be increased penalties for the unlawful behaviour. Corporate law itself should not be servant of the larger social goal of deterring crime. Instead, law compliance by corporate actors should be left to external enforcers, such as governmental regulators, criminal prosecutors and tort plaintiffs, there is no moral obligation to avoid illegal conduct when the corporation is willing to pay the price."[67]

Or, we have broken a law for our own benefit, now fine us and let us get on with making money. This cynical and amoral viewpoint is only tenable because of the lack of individual responsibility and does not extend to any other form of trading activity.

Our informed citizens (making a decision from behind a 'veil of ignorance') would be faced with the conflicting situations of a farmer who was jailed for four-and-a-half years when a young woman was tragically caught up in a tractor accident and died, and the fine of £80,000 imposed on a company when an employee was crushed beneath tons of grain. The difference is made more inexplicable when a similar accident at the company had already resulted in the death of another employee. They would be faced with a

---

[67] The Failure of Corporate Law, Greenfield (University of Chicago Press, 2006).

difficult moral decision, because of the discredited concept of legal personality. Should all similar cases simply be treated as unfortunate events and subject to a modest fine, or should an individual be held responsible where gross negligence is proved? Our informed citizens are clear: individual responsibility is necessary to help prevent future tragedies.

To ensure that laws are upheld, there are sanctions. For sanctions to be effective, they must be understood by, and be enforceable on, the perpetrator. The company is a piece of paper; responsibility for the upholding of the law is with the controlling management of the company. When in office, all power lies with the controlling management.

Our informed citizens would certainly wish this important condition written into law and into the formation documents of all companies for two reasons: firstly, on the basis of fairness, since all breaches of law should be treated equally; secondly, because allowing very large, economically dominant legal structures to be outside the normal legal sanctions risks encouraging and abetting law-breaking.

Second Principle
Legal responsibility extends to the Board of Management and senior management

By rejecting the concept of the corporate personality, the requirement for companies through their management to be subject to all relevant and current law is satisfied. More difficult is deciding who should be responsible for ensuring that compliance. That it must be human actors is unavoidable as otherwise responsibility does not exist.

In a democracy, citizens have both the right and the need to look behind the corporate veil to the human individuals directing the actions and assets of a company, as and when necessary. It is legitimate for them to require their government to identify and sanction their fellow citizens, or the citizens of another country, who are managing a company and who act illegally.

Before we can reach the next point of principle, we must examine what laws a company should be subject to in the interests of the citizen. The company does not exist physically but owning assets and undertaking activity always requires human assistance and direction to operate in the physical world. The managers and employees of a company are contractually bound, in return for financial reward, to carry out the instructions of the company as formulated by the board of directors. The company itself, as a fiction, can never formulate instructions, therefore it is always possible in the absence of the destruction of evidence or lying to identify who formulated and issued an instruction, and when. What is to prevent us from saying that all employees (or directors) of a company who break the law should be named and punished?

In this context, the legal requirement to retain documentation for six years is important. In the days of paper records this could be onerous but in today's electronic data era this should prove much easier and cheaper. All larger companies are audited every year, and the auditors' records supply another source of evidence. In the case of company collapse (liquidation or involuntary winding-up), it is difficult to justify why external bodies are forced to seek evidence, not always with the cooperation of management, for any failure. It is much more reasonable to expect the management to provide a detailed analysis of the circumstances leading to failure and that this document should be verified by the auditor. Who better to explain failure than those who have been involved in running the company day to day?

Penalties for failure to keep legally required financial information for the correct period should be commensurate with the seriousness of the failure. This requirement is already included in the Companies Act 2006 in paragraphs 386 to 389, but in typical British fashion, paragraph 387(2) states: "It is a defence for a person charged with such an offence to show that he acted honestly and that in the circumstances in which the company's business was carried on the default was excusable."

No other area of British law has the sort of 'get out' clauses which are to be found in company law, reflecting the 'good fellow' syndrome prevalent up to the present day.

Within a large company with thousands of individual employees, it can be almost impossible to identify an individual to punish. Should this prevent citizens from requiring their government to formulate rules (laws) which ensure that responsibility for illegal actions made in the name of a company, but in fact made by an individual, is carried by those responsible and sanctions applied? How is this to be effected? Starting with the principle that ignorance is no protection under the law, any individual who breaks a law is open to punishment, even if the illegal act was carried out at the nominal request of a company. A company cannot speak to issue orders, and in any event no individual can rely for a defence of an illegal act that someone else told them to do it.

Surely this solves the dilemma. Companies are subject to all the relevant laws of the land although, having no physical capacity, many laws governing human behaviour cannot be applied to them, only to their agent.

All managers at all levels contracted to manage a company therefore have to be able to demonstrate that they have taken all reasonable steps to ensure that they have appointed competent and qualified people to carry out all activities on behalf of the company and that there are clear instructions to all that every applicable law must be obeyed. Subject to this, they will be relieved of direct responsibility and the individual responsible for breaking any law will be held responsible. The government has already identified this necessity and codified it in detail in respect of banks.

But is a company entitled to do anything more than execute its legitimate business activities as mandated by its owners, the shareholders, and carried out by its directing minds, the management? Logic and a reference to democratic principles would dictate not. A company created as an entry in a Companies House file cannot have intent. It has capacity only to the extent that it has rights and responsibilities under the law but can have no rights under human rights legislation and can have no desire or need to propose or amend law

There is a dilemma here. Every qualifying citizen has the right to expect government to act on his or her behalf, but only as a citizen. The mechanism whereby citizens with common interests and objectives group together under an umbrella organisation to request government to act is well known, but in all cases the organisation is clearly a grouping of citizens with a common purpose (trades union, electoral reform society, political parties).

When the directors or senior management of a company, a legal fiction formed for a business purpose, address government, for whom are they speaking? We can discount the employees, unless a specific instruction has been received from each of them. Even less relevant are the shareholders. They must speak as citizens through other channels since, although they own a share of the assets of a company, they are completely divorced legally from that entity. This is also true of suppliers, the tax authorities, and the government, who only have a distant, legal relationship.

This must lead to the conclusion that the senior management of a company should confine its activities to meeting the financial commitments made to the shareholders and in ensuring that all the activities necessary to meet that requirement are conducted within existing law. This is, correctly, in a democracy, a narrow responsibility, and to exceed this narrow remit would be anti-democratic.

Current company law refers to the board of directors as having oversight over the activities of the company but places almost no direct responsibility on them.

I would prefer to use the term 'responsible management' to define what this group is and should be doing. In large groups of companies, board members are often appointed for a variety of reasons: some for their contacts, some as conduits to government or academia, and yet others to relay instructions from shareholders. This is all legitimate but outside what should be the true role of directors. If individuals appointed for non-controlling purposes are prepared to accept the risks and responsibilities of being a director, so be it.

Our informed citizens are now considering how such a Responsible Management should be structured and how its responsibilities should be defined. Luckily, in respect of banks, the government has already laid down some considerable detail.

The first logical assumption is that all directors are human beings. Having allowed limited liability to one company, the logic of another company represented by a human being sitting on the board is bizarre. This is again an example of the illogical steps which can be proposed when the concept of the legal personality is allowed to get out of control. The levels of illogicality which can be reached are displayed in the United Kingdom by the fact that whilst the stock exchange seeks to impose rules on quoted companies requiring the appointment of non-executive directors with experience, the Companies Act 2006 limits itself to requiring:

S154 (1) A private company must have at least one director.

(2) A public company must have at least two directors.

S155 (1) A company must have at least one director who is a natural person.

(2) This requirement is met if the office of director is held by a natural person as a corporation sole or otherwise by virtue of an office.

The glaring discrepancy between this requirement and how the government would wish banks to be managed is clear.

At present, we will limit ourselves to the principles surrounding company control. How would our informed citizens expect a major company to be controlled and managed to ensure that the requirement that actions carried out in the name of the company are legal and follow all relevant regulations? This is an enormous task and responsibility and requires skill and knowledge. The Responsible Management must ensure that the company has the structure and knowledge base to be able to comply with this requirement. Our informed citizens would wish to allocate the ultimate responsibility to individuals making up the controlling management, which may extend beyond the formal Board of Directors.

Limited liability may restrict the financial losses of investors to the capital injected but cannot be stretched to imply that illegal actions of a company cannot be pursued, and sanctions imposed on those individuals responsible for precisely preventing this.

This concept of responsibility cascades down through the company. The board of directors has two overarching tasks: to state clearly that it is the intention of the company management that all activities of the company comply with the law and all relevant regulations, and to ensure that sufficient resources are allocated to achieving this end and are available to all employees tasked with managing the company's activities. If the company cannot safely oversee and fund its activities, those activities must cease.

On this basis, the present requirements of the Companies Act are inadequate. Public companies and large private companies should have a management board of sufficient size and experience to enable each major sector of the business to be the responsibility of a designated director. For such key areas as law/taxation, employment and health and safety, it is not unreasonable to expect that person to have the necessary training and experience to adequately supervise the relevant sector. These positions should be identified as having this responsibility and, moreover, the responsibility to follow all relevant laws. There is certainly a strong argument for proposing that for large companies an absolute minimum of six directors is needed and, for all other companies, three. If the responsible positions are not board position, they should be officially named and reported.

The position in respect of corporate criminal and regulatory responsibility in the United Kingdom at present is at best confused and confusing. In response to the Law Commission Discussion Paper on Corporate Criminal Responsibility, the Bar Council in its response said, "However, that there is a need to act and make such a choice is not, in our view, really in doubt. Such a need is clearly mandated by the current failure of the law on corporate criminal liability properly to deal with crimes allegedly committed by larger corporations."

In England and Wales, there are three ways a corporate can be prosecuted for a criminal offence committed by those acting on its behalf:

1. If Parliament has created a specific criminal offence for corporates, such as under the Bribery Act 2010 or the Criminal Finances Act 2017.

2. Through vicarious liability, which is generally used for regulatory offences that do not require proof of fault.

3. Through the identification doctrine, when someone who can be said to be the 'directing mind and will' of a corporate commits the offence. [Commons Library Research Briefing, June 27th, 2022]

An example of the sort of criminal offence targeted by the Criminal Finance Act 2017 would be the prosecution of tax evasion. It establishes the corporate criminal offence of failing to prevent the facilitation of tax evasion. A defence would be available for corporates who could show that they had reasonable procedures in place to avoid such an event. This illustrates perfectly the illogicality of the law when it conflates the company with individuals employed to run it and which are employed by it. The intent of the act is clear: to enable the prosecution to take place and to try to recover lost tax. Because of the difficulty of identifying individuals who may have authorised the evasion, better to prosecute the company. If, however, we postulate that the company must obey all laws, the company's management will have to take steps to ensure that its tax affairs are in the hands of competent people, who are quite clearly instructed to obey all laws. Under these circumstances, an employee can have no incentive to carry out an illegal act unless for their own personal gain, which would be a criminal act against the company. It is in the company's interest to identify and prosecute that individual. The only alternative is that the owners/managers of the company authorised the act and therefore they should be prosecuted personally.

This leads us to the third way a company can be prosecuted, through the identification doctrine, which has been interpreted narrowly by the courts. By requiring that only the most senior persons can be the 'directing mind and will' of a company, it is arguable that large companies are let off the hook, since many key decisions will be decentralised away from the most senior management.

The result is that the application of the identification principle makes it easier to prosecute small and medium-sized companies, rather than large companies with complex domestic and international management structures. The Bar Council very carefully noted, "We are not in a position to comment on the prevalence, if at all, of companies arranging their internal structures and communications so as to evade prosecution via the identification principle. The current route to criminal liability does though allow for such an approach." (Bar Council response to the Law Commission Discussion Paper on Corporate Criminal Liability)

The fact is that companies internally are quite clear who has authority at different levels to enact company business. United Kingdom company law and practice has never found it necessary to externally define levels of authority, unlike in Germany.

This answers the question raised by our informed citizens about how the responsibility already in place for individuals can be extended to the complex world of the company.

There is no intent to seek scapegoats, and in particular no intent to open a company to malicious litigation. Accidents happen despite the best efforts of individuals. It is sufficient for the exoneration of a company's Board of Directors or responsible management to show that instruction and resources were in place. If further down the management structure an individual had deliberately decided to breach instructions (if all else is in place an unlikely event, as there can be no advantage in such an act except for criminal intent), responsibility can be placed where it belongs.

Third Principle
Interaction between the company and the state must be transparent

The third principle which our informed citizens insist on is that interaction between the state and the company should be transparent. This is particularly relevant where private companies take public money to supply services or goods. Can commercial confidentiality and the correct use of public money co-exist? It did not in the past; some of the great fortunes of the 18th and early 19th centuries were made by politicians and their enablers having control of public funds. Recent experience shows an unwelcome return to this situation.

The legal myth reinvented and perpetuated by successive legal decisions over the last 150 years has lulled citizen and lawmaker into giving human attributes to the company. Human beings, as citizens, have a right to privacy, and to the protection of human rights law, but the legal construct, the company, does not. This is not to say that that its affairs should be opened to scrutiny completely but that, where there is a conflict between the requirements of the state and its citizens for transparency, the rights of the state should have precedence. Some confusion also creeps into the equation from the protection human rights law gives to private property. It is difficult to find the justification for applying this concept to the company. The controlling management's income and remuneration is private and dealt with in their personal tax affairs. This is also true of the owners of the company, the members or shareholders. But is the degree of proprietorial ownership of the company sufficient for their rights to be protected by human rights law?

The traditional view of the shareholder is as owner of the company. The company should serve the shareholders first because the company belongs to them. The leading proponent of the property-based argument is Milton Friedman who once popularised the claim that "the one and only social responsibility of business is to increase its profits". The argument that ownership does not protect the owner from regulation is especially strong regarding corporations. Shareholders, even if they are best seen as owners of the firm, already have fewer ownership 'rights' than any other kind of owner.

"The slice of the ownership of a company provided by one's share ownership is, at best, the most attenuated of any property claim. For example, a shareholder's 'ownership' does not give her the right of access to the company's place of business, the right to exclude others from the property, the right to decide the use of the property on a day-to-day basis, or practically any other right usually associated with ownership of a piece of property. So even if shareholders are considered owners of the corporation, in order to use such ownership as an argument against corporate reform one would need a much more sophisticated defence of why such ownership gives absolute power to shareholders when it does not provide such protection in other settings."[68]

As Professor Greenfield has stated, "no prominent contemporary corporate law scholar uses property rights as the primary rationale for shareholder dominance. Even the more conservative law and economics scholars have abandoned property rights as the basis of corporate law doctrine or theory." [69]

The informed citizen may well conclude that the member/shareholder's personal privacy is protected by his

---

[68]Greenfield, The Failure of Corporate Law, (University of Chicago Press, 2006).
[69] Ibid.

or her private tax and business affairs but that in respect of the internal workings of the company, ownership of the residual profit and capital of the company does not override the requirement for transparency of what is a legal construct. How far might this transparency extend? Whilst there is an argument for commercial confidentiality between two companies engaged in their private negotiations, where the state is financially involved or has a material strategic interest, the requirements of transparency require that any contractual arrangements are open to public scrutiny. Equally, a company, as a legal fiction, can scarcely wish its tax affairs to be confidential and the management of the company will also wish to assure their shareholders and their fellow citizens that the requirements of tax laws have been followed.

Fourth Principle
There is an absolute prohibition on company involvement in politics

Our fourth principle is the easiest to state: there is an absolute prohibition on political activity and on financial donations to political parties, either directly or indirectly, by a company, which by extension involves a similar prohibition for the board of management, the shareholders, and on employees of the company when acting in that capacity. There should be severe penalties for breaching this prohibition.

There is no need to qualify this; the company is outside the political sphere because it is a legal construct allowed by the citizens through their government for specific commercial purposes only with a special level of protection not available elsewhere. All the company must do is follow all applicable law as democratically approved by the citizens.

The board of management and employees are not deprived of any political rights by this prohibition; they are simply placed in the same position as all others, and for this reason this principle will be readily approved by the informed citizen, who will be only too aware of the potential for economic blackmail by an economically important company over the state and its citizens.

Any attempt by a representative of a company to influence government or legislation is anti-democratic, since it cannot be established on whose behalf they are speaking, except their own.

Government does need accurate and timely information to aid the formulation of policy and usually obtains it from published financial information and national statistics from a variety of sources. Transparent groupings of companies by sector to collate and supply accurate information to government may be allowed.

However, the reverse is not true. Citizens, or groups of citizens, have every right to instruct, within the democratic framework, to amend or introduce new laws to regulate or in any way change the status of companies (which have no human rights) and to regulate their activities and place any demands on the directors and senior managers always, in this case, subject to human rights law.

This has profound implications for the modern state. Government has a duty to listen to any citizen or, more practically, any group of citizens, who wish to influence legislation.

If, as an individual, you choose to invest your money in a company, you are free to lobby, as are all citizens, for any legal change, if necessary to suit your invested company. The company cannot. It has no political voice.

It is the role of a director to ensure that the commercial business is run for the benefit of the shareholders. This may involve taking legal action on existing contracts but can never extend to having a political opinion on behalf of a legal fiction. The legal fiction simply must operate within the legal framework agreed by the citizens of the country in which it is incorporated. The only legitimate claim would be equality of treatment, i.e. all laws should apply equally to all similar companies.

Fifth Principle
Large, economically important companies and companies supplying socially necessary services will be subject to added control and scrutiny

Another matter of concern to our informed citizens is that of the company which is of such a size, or which occupies such a sensitive commercial or social sector, that its mismanagement or failure could have a material negative effect on a specific group of citizens, a region, or on the country as a whole. We have already seen how endemic this is in Britain. The two issues, sensitivity and size, need to be considered separately. Companies for a social purpose should be controlled whatever their size. The cut-off point for additional control because a company may be so big that its failure or material change may have a profound effect on a country or region is more difficult to define and will have to be arbitrary. All governments are concerned by this but generally take no pre-emptive legal steps to equip themselves with potential solutions, and citizens in general have a fatalistic view that nothing can be done to mitigate any problems caused by this issue. This is in part because of the belief that as private property the owners can do what they wish, when they like, with a company.

We have already seen that the private company has many weaknesses when asked to take on the role of government, not least the danger of 'financialization' and the need to recover investments far more quickly than the life of an asset would require, inevitably costing the citizen more than necessary and at worst not providing essential services.

Although the traditional view, still held by right-wing legal theorists, this is increasingly challenged in modern legal theory. We have already seen that the ownership rights of shareholders of a company are so limited as to be little more than the right to a dividend where justified and to the balance of capital on a liquidation. Set against these limited rights is the wellbeing of the direct employees, the suppliers to the company and their employees and the local infrastructure which a major company supports, and which supports it. Professor Greenfield, quoting Blair and Stout, notes: "shareholders are not the only group that provides essential, specialised inputs into public corporations. Bond owners own their bonds, suppliers own their inventory, and workers 'own' their labour. Each of these owners contributes property to the corporate enterprise not as a charitable act but as an investment from which each expects to make some profitable return. Further, the input of each is essential to the success of the firm. To say that shareholders are the only 'owners' is to say that there is something inherent in the act of contributing money to buy shares – or in the definition of 'ownership' of shares – to distinguish that act from the contribution of money to buy bonds issued by the company, the supply of raw materials to be refined by the company, or the investment of human labour to be used by the company...

"The dominant contemporary paradigm in corporate law depends on contract principles. The modern theory of the firm tells us that, while each participant in the corporate enterprise owns certain inputs (labour, capital, machinery, inventory), the firm itself is nothing but a web of contractual relationships among these production factors."[70]

Our informed citizens, aware of the factors surrounding the firm but not knowing their role in society, would recognise and empathise with this interpretation of the company and with the logical conclusions which stem from it. They will recognise too that there has been considerable investment over long periods, often inter-generational, by

---

[70] Greenfield, The Failure of Corporate Law, (University of Chicago Press, 2006).

many participants, and that the state must put into place measures to inhibit sudden, damaging change.

We will look at more remedies for this risk later but the first is the need for ongoing capital adequacy in all companies and the granting of limited liability only to the holding company. In the case of a large company not in danger of immediate collapse, the legal requirement for timely transparency on planned changes and the requirement for a social plan to cushion any blow to employees is the minimum legal requirement to place on a company. This must be a legal requirement with serious penalties to remove risk of economic extortion with the threat to create economic chaos if the companies' plans are not accommodated. One requirement for the special case of social provision by private companies is that a single form of incorporation covering all situations would be too limiting.

At the beginning of the 21st century, we have effectively one form of company, divided into private and public formats but differing in principle only on the degree of regulation and disclosure required of them. This is too narrow a view, inadequate for the modern mixed economy and providing too little oversight of the key activities of major companies which affect the citizen either because of their size and dominance or because their object is to supply essential services to the citizen. To differentiate possible types of company necessary to cover differing social requirements, it will be vital to reintroduce a number of legal requirements previously considered essential in company law, but which have been systematically removed to allow companies total freedom to operate however their directors choose.

There is a minimum requirement for four types of company. In addition to the equivalent of the present PLC and private limited company, the modern mixed economy also requires a public social company and a private social company. The PuSC would be formed where a social service is conducted by a private company using any public funds (an example would be The West Yorkshire Community Rehabilitation Company Limited discussed earlier), the PriSC where a social service is carried out by a private company without any call on public funds (including guarantees) as typified by Thames Water. In the case of these companies, the old concept of ultra vires (the requirement for a company to be created for a specific purpose and keep to it) needs to make a comeback as designated and necessary social companies should have their activities limited to that for which they were set up in order to ring-fence them financially and to prevent speculation with public money or risk to vulnerable citizens. Again, we will have to return later to develop this principle as it is tied up with protection of capital and the role of the subsidiary company.

In simple terms, should citizens at some point in the future vote democratically to take an operation into public ownership, one option would be to buy the company shares at a fair market value from the shareholders.

If the state decides to allow private operation of, for example, such a key function as the care of the elderly, the citizens must be assured of two things. All funds supplied must be used exclusively and beneficially for that purpose, and the whole operation must retain integrity and cohesion.

There will, in future, be changes in political perception of how social services are funded and operated. It is essential for future democracy that such changes are not hindered, or even completely prevented, by legal constraints.

Sixth Principle
All companies must be, and remain, adequately capitalised

Share Capital is the amount of money which the shareholders (owners) put into the company initially to fund the business and is the amount they would lose were the company to fail. The level of share capital in a company is important as it represents a financial commitment to the company by the owners, provides a reason for them not to close the company on a whim, and gives security to anyone doing business with the company. The amount of share capital should also, logically, increase with the size of the company as the security provided by a multi-million-pound company with a share capital of £100 is derisory. This concept is accepted by the company laws of many countries (see Germany, Switzerland and particularly China) and is built into their law. Britain is almost unique in having a company law which pays little attention to the capitalisation of companies with the inevitable damage which this brings.

Our informed citizens would not find this requirement unreasonable as they have, as citizens, already conferred a huge benefit on the company and its shareholders; that of limited liability. It is, therefore, not unreasonable that legal requirements are placed on a company to ensure that it has sufficient capital to avoid a collapse. What are the current requirements of company law? The answer is, as usual, little. As a result of European Union influence, the Companies Act 2006 includes in Section 763 (1) "The authorised minimum" in relation to the nominal value of a public companies allotted share capital is -

(a) £50,000 or
(b) the prescribed Euro equivalent.

In the Companies Act 2006, the familiar concept of authorised capital was abolished and the requirement to state a company's share capital in its constitution ceased. For private companies, therefore, however large and economically important, the share capital is what the founders decide. At what level the capital of the company is maintained is also not legislated for.

The extensive Part 17, with eighteen chapters and 118 sections on A Company's Share Capital, does not include any requirement for large and socially and/or nationally important companies to maintain an adequate capital base.

A private limited company in Britain should have a minimum share capital of £20,000, of which at least £5,000 should be paid in cash on formation, with no possibility to pay in kind, that is using existing assets. To protect both the citizen or company who may have dealings with the new company and to protect the owners, when 50% of the total share capital (£20,000) is gone the company would call a shareholders meeting and when the share capital is no longer available the company must declare insolvency. The purpose of this is to reduce the hundreds of thousands of companies set up and liquidated each year which the authorities have no capacity to monitor.

There are provisions in the Act to regulate dividend distributions.

Section 830 (1) A company may only make a distribution out of profits available for the purpose, defined as its net accumulated, realised profits.

Section 831 (1) A public company may only make a distribution -

(a) if the amount of its net assets is not less than the aggregate of its called-up capital and undistributable reserves [that is it is not insolvent]**, and**

(b) if, and to the extent that the distribution does not reduce the amount of those assets to less than that aggregate.

This may seem complex, but our informed citizens can see the implications at once. For a private company, however large, there is nothing to stop the management and shareholders stripping out all accumulated reserves and leaving the company under-capitalised and therefore dependent on external borrowing, with the risk that this might be withdrawn. Those readers who may wonder whether this could happen and what the effect might be should recall (in addition to some of the examples given previously such as ICI, P+O, British Oxygen, Pilkington's Glass and General Electric) the demise of BHS.

To protect the state and its citizens, all companies should have a minimum capital requirement which increases as the company grows, in the form of share capital and undistributable reserves at least equivalent to a percentage of the company's total assets.

It is always useful to see how other, successful, European countries regulate company capital; in particular Germany, which has a strong corporate base. The German GmbH law states that the share capital cannot fall below that established on the formation of the company. When the share capital is reduced by a half, the law requires that a meeting of all shareholders is called. When the share capital is no longer available, under Paragraph 64 of the GmbHG (GmbH Law) the company must declare insolvency.

A similar requirement should be included in any revised United Kingdom company law, applying to all companies, including subsidiary companies. If a parent company cannot maintain the capital adequacy of a subsidiary company, there must be doubt concerning the stability of the whole group.

Another successful European country is Switzerland. Greatly simplified, Swiss company law makes a clear distinction between capital reserves (reserves which cannot be distributed as dividends to the owners) and retained earnings; to the capital reserve are allocated the proceeds obtained from the issue of shares in excess of the nominal value and the issue costs. Any part of the statutory capital reserve which, together with the statutory retained earnings less any losses, exceeds half of the registered share capital may be repaid to the shareholders. Five per cent of the annual profit must be allocated to the statutory retained earnings. The statutory retained earnings must be accumulated until they have reached, together with the statutory capital reserve, the amount of 50% of the registered share capital. Holding companies must accumulate statutory retained earnings until they reach, together with the statutory capital reserves, 20% of the registered share capital. A strengthened version of this law would provide a sound starting point for the drafting of similar requirements in a revised British company law.

It is illuminating to compare this with the, again greatly simplified, situation in the United Kingdom, where a private company can distribute its 'accumulated, realised profits' in full if it so wishes.

Many successful European countries have a more conservative and citizen-friendly attitude to capital adequacy for companies and countries which can be viewed as competitors and seek to attract foreign capital do not hesitate to ensure that foreign inward investment brings with it sufficient capital. As an example, the capital necessary to form a Foreign Invested Company in China is extremely high and will be a percentage of the proposed investment but in any event, unlike in the UK, will be many millions of pounds.

This is relevant also in the context of foreign direct investment, where it is common to see this in the form of substantial investment in productive capacity, as with Nissan in Sunderland, Toyota in Derby, and Honda in Swindon. (Honda in Swindon did not close its production facilities because of capital or taxation requirements but in part because the United Kingdom left the European Union). Such major, reputable companies are not put off by reasonable requirements relating to capital and taxation; they are quite used to it in many parts of the world. Much of China's economic growth over the last thirty years has been because of this sort of foreign direct investment from Europe and the United States of America.

Potentially more dangerous is the foreign direct investment which buys up already existing companies and extracts their economic value before either selling them on or closing them down. An example would be the purchase of British Leyland by SAIC Motor Corporation of China, where the production machinery was dismantled, moved to China, and used to produce British-branded cars for export to Britain.

Seventh Principle
All companies must pay a fair and proportionate amount of tax

The taxation of companies and its history in the United Kingdom is too complex to be covered in any detail, but two areas of company taxation are worth explaining.

The first is the possibility for companies, in certain circumstances, to carry back trading losses to offset against tax paid in earlier years, and in most circumstances to carry forward trading and other losses to offset against future tax liability. In the case of a group of companies these losses can be moved around relatively freely. In addition, companies can offset capital investment (the purchase of assets to use in the business) against current taxation, thereby deferring tax liabilities into the future. Deferred tax is defined as being the amount of income tax payable in future periods in respect of temporary timing differences so, in simple terms, deferred tax is tax that is payable in the future. The presumed purpose of this deferral is to encourage companies to invest their capital in productive assets to create future profits. This negates the argument that taxation discourages companies from investing, as the opposite is true: invest and you have the possibility to defer tax; if you continue to invest at the same level, the tax deferral will continue.

The second area of relevance is the existence of group relief and consortium relief, both of which are complex areas of corporate taxation, but which deserve a brief, simple outline. Group relief means that HMRC treats groups of companies as one economic unit for corporation tax purposes and allows one company to surrender its tax losses to another company in the group to offset against that company's taxable profit. The ownership threshold is 75% or above. At first sight this seems reasonable, but groups of companies may form an economic unit and be tightly integrated, or they may simply be a grouping of disparate companies under one ownership, any one of them capable of being bought, sold, or allowed to fail at any time. (This lends further argument to Principle 8, that limited liability should not extend to subsidiary companies.) Group relief may also be available where the surrendering company is owned by a consortium, the claimant company is also a member of the consortium, and both the companies are based in the UK.

This is an even more complex area of tax, which was introduced mainly to aid British shipping companies in the 1970s, who had set up consortia where trading companies are owned by a holding company, which itself has many owners, after the introduction of containerisation. After being merged, bought and sold, by 2006 none of the companies for whom this relief was designed existed, all having been taken over by foreign companies.

From having the largest container fleet in Europe in the 1970s, Britain now has virtually none and its businesses have been absorbed into Danish, French, German and Swiss/Italian fleets, which dominate world containerised shipping. This shows yet again that levels and structures of corporate taxation play at best a marginal role in the success or failure of companies and the demise of British container shipping was the result of a variety of factors, many home-grown, of which taxation was not one.

How much tax it is just (continuing with our concept of justice) for companies to pay varies over time. Until 1965, company taxation was at the same rate as income tax rates for individual citizens. In 1949, for example, the taxation rate for individuals and companies was 50%, with an added profits tax on companies. When introduced in 1965, Corporation Tax was 40%, increased in 1969 to 45%, and put back to 40% in 1972. From 1973 to 1982, the rate of

Corporation Tax was 52% (with a reduced rate for small companies) until beginning to fall steadily to 30% in 1999, remaining at this rate until 2007. It has been government policy since then to continually reduce the Corporation Tax rate, down to a level of 19% in 2017. Only recently, because of the pandemic, has it been proposed to raise the rate, to 25%.

All this goes to prove that the rate of corporation tax is driven by political ideology (derived from economic theory) and that, given that the period 1945 to 1970 was one of high growth, corporation tax rates do not stimulate or hinder economic development. Companies invest where they see profit potential and disinvest where the opposite is true. Equally, companies outside the 'turbo-capitalism' genre with long-term plans and embedded in the community appreciate that their success also depends on the surrounding infrastructure of transport, education, health and security, and that this benefit also has a cost.

When asked what level of taxation a company should pay, our informed citizens will reply: the same as we do. This calculation is not as easy as it sounds (and was correct at the time of writing but may now no longer be). The basic rate of income tax is 20%, rising to 40% on incomes over £50,000, with personal allowances reducing the headline rate. Equally, this takes no account of VAT where citizens pay a tax of 20% on most purchases; for companies, this is not a tax but a throughput. Whilst income tax is payable by all citizens (residents), shareholders in a company may well not be citizens of the country in which the company is registered and does its business. It is therefore important that the revenue necessary to support the state infrastructure is collected in full, directly from the company.

For the citizen in the United Kingdom earning £40,000, the effective tax rate is 24.8% and for those earning over £100,000, the rate is 34.3%. These rates of course ignore

VAT. Our informed citizens would suggest that the fair treatment of a company would be for all companies to pay tax at a rate of 25% on taxable profits up to £100,000 and at a rate of 34% on taxable profits over £100,000.

As well as adequate capitalisation, we have also considered other changes to company law, in particular the role of subsidiary companies, as well as the role of management and its exclusion from politics. More difficult to encompass within company law, but essential to regulate, is the need for companies both to pay a fair level of tax and, equally importantly, to ensure that wealth generated by companies is not transferred offshore either tax-free or with an unrealistically low level of tax paid. This requirement has nothing to do with human rights.

Justice in fairness proposes that the life opportunities and experiences of the most disadvantaged in society can be improved by a modest increase in income and the societal safety net. Because in modern, Western, industrial society – particularly in the United Kingdom – there are a lot of these disadvantaged people, the sum required by government is large. It is also a measured and reported fact that the amounts of tax revenue lost to government by failure to collect due taxes and by the, apparently legal, transfer of untaxed income offshore is also large.

The ability in the past to deduct all interest cost from profits had a double negative effect on UK corporate activity. It encouraged companies, in the period of shareholder value, to replace equity (share capital) with borrowing to improve the return on equity and, even more damagingly, it encouraged the takeover of profitable companies funded solely by debt, effectively enabling the acquisition of a company using its own cash flow. Since the acquirer still wanted or needed income, this usually meant loading the acquired company with additional debt (borrowings) to fund the payment of dividends. Many healthy UK companies have been driven into eventual liquidation by these methods.

This danger was reduced following the introduction of the UK Corporate Interest Restriction 'CIR' rules, which came into effect on April 1st 2017. These regulations were not introduced solely on the initiative of the UK government but followed from an initiative by the OECD59 and the G20, begun some years earlier. These measures were introduced in the UK with a 30% limit on interest deductions and complex procedures for calculating a multinational group worldwide interest deduction allowance, coupled with a de minimis amount of £2 million pounds below which no controls applied. It is to be hoped that these rules will impact leveraged acquisitions.

Our informed citizen should not have a difficult choice to make in respect of corporate tax. Under a fair system, as a disadvantaged member of society our citizen could expect a living income and a secure safety net and, should they be a successful entrepreneur, they should still have a substantial income, even if somewhat lower than before. Our informed citizen can see the logic in choosing the just option.

This choice is of course only logical under the conditions previously postulated. The entrepreneur, if aware of his or her position, would be outraged at their reduced income and probably quote human rights law. Here is strong argument for the justice in the use of the modified contract theory, as the downside of this is felt by the entrepreneur who, instead of being extremely rich, is now only rich. His or her lifestyle, encompassing health and general legal and societal rights, has not been materially affected. Had earlier avenues to avoid tax not been open, our entrepreneur would have been quite happy with his or her wealth. Only to have an existing tax avoidance route removed causes upset.

Of course, by acting through a limited company, the profits never belonged to our entrepreneur in the first place. The profits were those of the company, which quite reasonably is required to pay a fair amount of tax for all the advantages of operating securely in a democracy. There will, of course, be objections: what about the small businessperson with a £2 company and a modest turnover? Surely, they are extremely unlikely to be transferring royalties and interest offshore, this a complex and expensive undertaking. One could also ask, what about the large private and public company with many shareholders and a management acting on their behalf? Nothing changes in principle because there is more than one 'entrepreneur'.

One final thought. Governments should look at similar, successful economies and consider what they may be doing to improve their tax take and emulate it. One such economy is Germany, which has the concept of 'Betriebspruefung', or business audit for tax purposes. In addition to the usual tax civil servants, the tax authorities employ a large team of external, experienced, and expert tax auditors to visit businesses at regular and varying intervals, to review their tax position. Businesses are divided into small, medium and large, and visit intervals vary depending on size. Small business visits are by their nature infrequent, medium more so, and larger quite regular. The turnover and profit levels defining medium and large businesses is quite low: to be defined as large requires a turnover of €8.6 million and a profit of €335,000 for a commercial business, with €5.2 million and a profit of €300,000 for an industrial business. Middle-sized businesses are visited on average every eleven years and the previous three years are checked, while large businesses are checked on an ongoing basis for the previous six years.

The success of this system can be seen in the official nationwide results for 2019. 13,341 auditors visited 181,345 businesses and produced additional revenue of €15.2 billion. Considering the frequency of visits and the large number of applicable businesses, this can be assumed to be an ongoing result. What cannot be measured is the pressure on businesses to ensure that their tax calculations are as correct as possible, to avoid having to explain why a large, subsequent correction has proved necessary. With an estimated UK tax gap of £35 billion per year, it is legitimate to wonder why a United Kingdom government does not introduce a similar system.

A similar level of wonder can be directed at Britain's lack of a dividend-withholding tax. Many other countries apply them, and Germany again supplies an example. German companies paying dividends (also interest and royalties, but we will stay with dividends for now) deduct a dividend-withholding tax of 25% and a solidarity surcharge of 5%, giving an effective deduction of a little over 26%. Corporate recipients of dividends can apply for a refund of the tax withheld over the corporation tax rate of 15% plus solidarity surcharge, regardless of any further relief available under a double tax treaty. This may not seem of importance but assumes considerable relevance when the list of countries having a double tax treaty with Germany is reviewed. Conspicuous by their absence are tax havens such as the British Virgin Islands and similar British dependencies. Double tax agreements should benefit both countries, but it is difficult to identify what advantage Britain would have agreeing a tax treaty, including dividend tax relief, with a tax haven. Everything goes one way.

Governments collect tax from citizens and bodies which benefit from the infrastructure of the modern state (including companies) and have the ability and power to do so effectively and comprehensively. If the British government were to collect taxes due, at a reasonable level, in full of activity (productive) within Britain, an adequate level of government income would be assured.

In a complex modern democracy, funding those sectors of society which the citizen has to make use of, and which are by general agreement best funded consensually by taxation, the contribution which a company should make to this general good is open to debate as to the appropriate level, but not to the principle of contribution. Although only a vehicle for commercial activity created by legal agreement, the shareholders of the company gain from all this public provision in exactly the same way as its human citizens as, without healthy, educated employees and a suitable public infrastructure, the company remains a name on a piece of paper, and totally incapable of generating any profit for its shareholders.

Eighth Principle
Limited Liability does not extend to subsidiary companies

We have touched on two consistent themes in company law: the concept of corporate personality, and the fact that much of the law under which companies are regulated is not statute law but case law. These two themes are intricately linked and best seen in the extension of the concept of limited liability beyond the intention of the original concept and far beyond a level which our informed citizens would find acceptable or logical. Although the citizens through the state may agree that the granting of limited liability may make sense to the providers of risk capital for a new or expanding commercial venture, they would have no reason to agree with the idea that this concession should be extended to all companies, in particular to the subsidiary company of another company, when that parent company is adequately funded and capable of meeting the liabilities of its subsidiary.

The parent corporation is not an absentee owner; therefore, avoidance of exposure to risk of absentee investors is not a relevant factor. Because the parent corporation is the sole shareholder, the necessity of limited liability to encourage the widespread distribution of shares (a requirement for very large enterprises) is also irrelevant. The parent company facing the risk of liability for the debts of its subsidiaries is in a position to diversify its portfolio and spread the risk. Economists recognise that a similar ability to diversify on the part of financial institutions which are ultimate investors would make the imposition of limited liability significantly less important than in the case of individual investors lacking the ability to diversify. This factor would be as applicable to corporate groups as to financial institutions.[71]

In summary, most, but not all, of the suggested arguments for limited liability simply do not apply to corporate groups or at least are not always fully applicable. The extension of layers of limited liability to the tiers of subsidiaries within corporate groups lacks most of the theoretical justification that has been advanced in defence of the rule. So, reconsideration of the rule is in order, particularly since application of limited liability to corporate groups appears to have been accidental. (Blumberg, 1986)

It is important to understand why the legitimacy of the assumption that tiers of wholly owned subsidiaries, each with limited liability, is challenged, and the implications of its existence fully appreciated. There are serious repercussions for the citizen, both in terms of physical risk and potential huge financial cost in allowing this structure to go unregulated.

"Over the last ten years, the ownership of an increasing number of nuclear plants has been transferred to a relatively small number of very large corporations. These large corporations have adopted business structures that create separate limited liability subsidiaries for each nuclear plant and, in a number of instances, separate operating and ownership entities that provide additional liability buffers between the nuclear plant and its ultimate owners. The limited liability structures being utilised are effective mechanisms for transferring profits to the parent/owner while avoiding tax payments. They also provide a financial shield for the parent/owner if an accident, equipment failure, safety upgrade, or unusual maintenance need at one plant creates a large, unanticipated cost. The

---

[71] Limited Liability and Corporate Groups, Phillip Blumberg, University of Connecticut Law School, 1986.

parent/owner can walk away, by declaring bankruptcy for that separate unit, without jeopardising its other nuclear and non-nuclear investments."[72]

This is potentially a dangerous situation and one which is readily recognisable in Britain; no-one need be responsible for complex and potentially dangerous technology, and the pressure is considerably lessened when it is possible to simply walk away from all liability. Anyone wishing to understand the implications of this should study the Bhopal tragedy in India, where a chemical plant owned by a subsidiary of a US company exploded, killing immediately around 20,000 people and injuring tens of thousands of others, with long-term effects. The US company abandoned the plant, subsidiary and the people and left, hence no compensation or assistance.

Provided the principles above are adhered to, in respect of adequate capitalisation, no subsidiary should be so weak as to require liquidation or be beyond the resources of its parent company to fund. The principle that limited liability can only be claimed once is necessary to prevent the potential abuse of economic power by management in allowing limited liability for subsidiary companies. Having set up a subsidiary company, the management of the parent company can set the level of capital, borrowing, and the addition or removal of assets and liabilities so that the subsidiary company is not a separate economic unit. The idea that as a separate corporate personality the subsidiary company is entitled to limited liability is an abuse of the system and an example of the perverse consequences of accepting the discredited concept of corporate personality.

---

[72] Stephanie Blankenburg, Dan Plesch and Frank Wilkinson. Cambridge Journal of Economics, 2010, 821-836. Limited Liability and the Modern Corporation in Theory and Practice.

Chapter 14
A New Approach to Regulating Companies

The points of principle that should underpin changes to United Kingdom company law apply only to companies incorporated under British company law. As far as British law is concerned, "The general principle is that the provisions in the Companies Acts do not apply extra territorially. This reflects the general stance of English law."[73] There are limited exceptions to this rule in respect of insolvent companies but in general the rule holds. To make the same point from a reverse direction, British law can regulate companies formed in Britain, but companies incorporated abroad, even if subsidiaries of a British holding company, are subject to the laws of the country of incorporation. This is what you would expect but it is often forgotten or overlooked in the study of multinational and transnational groups.

Our point of principle that limited liability does not extend to subsidiary companies can therefore only apply to, and be enforced in, Britain.

Does this matter? In principle it would be ideal if this could be extended to all companies but practically this is clearly not possible and does not negate the objective of changing British company law to benefit the citizens of this country. The citizens of other countries may, where this is possible, wish to pressure their own government to make similar principled changes to company law, but this does not prevent British changes.

Why is this change so important? As we have seen, the promulgators of company law saw the advantage in

---

[73] National Corporate Law in a Globalised Market, David Millman. Edward Elgar 2009.

encouraging investors to finance business ventures, some of which may be risky, with the considerable advantage of limited liability. This had in part the effect of transferring risk to other participants, creditors and today other contracted parties, including the government for tax owed and employees for wages and salaries (and for tax deducted but not paid over to the government), but this was considered a valuable trade-off. Only through the judicial acceptance of the concept of corporate personality and its extension into the relationship between holding and subsidiary companies did this initial concession become extended to all companies.

The importance and effect of these decisions is noted by Millman. "One pervasive consequence of the principle is that where there is a group of companies, all companies within the group are viewed as distinct entities, each with their own rights and liabilities. This means that parent companies can avoid many liabilities of their subsidiaries unless they have explicitly guaranteed their obligations. This logical application of the Salomon rule to a secondary level is valued highly by the international commercial interests and is the bedrock on which the multinational corporation exists... In this latter instance (Adams v Cape Industries, 1990, BCLC 479), the Court of Appeal confirmed that there is nothing improper in an international group of companies structuring their business affairs in such a way as to reduce the exposure of the parent company to risk by insulating it from the potential liabilities of subsidiaries operating in another state. Multinationals are thus able to use subsidiaries to generate profits (which will be remitted to the holding company as dividends) in high-risk jurisdictions, without worrying about the attendant liabilities."[74]

---

[74] National Corporate Law in a Globalised Market, David Millman. Edward Elgar 2009.

These judgements are no justification for extending limited liability to British subsidiaries. Any risk can only come from bad management or fraud. In any event, we have already seen that removal of the concession cannot be extended to overseas subsidiaries.

Irrespective of whether we are dealing with one large company, a national group of companies, or an international group of companies, it is important that governments, on behalf of their citizens, regulate those companies registered and operating within their borders, irrespective of the fact that they cannot do the same for companies registered and operating outside their borders. We are dealing, therefore, now with the regulation of British companies. We will look later at the implications throughout the rest of the world.

A combination of the principle of adequate capitalisation of all companies together with the removal of limited liability from subsidiary companies would remove an unwarrantedly powerful and unnecessary tool from company management. This would place responsibility where it belongs, with the managing board of the parent company, and negate the situation where this management can direct the activities of a subsidiary company but at any time step back from all responsibility. It would be comforting to think that Principles 1 and 2 would obviate the need for this step but the reality of the power structure within groups of companies means that this is unlikely.

Corporate Interests

An oft-repeated theme when discussing reform of company law is that no government can risk acting against powerful corporate interests. This has never been true, but examples of action are rare and, unusually enough, not recent. The concept of commercial transactions taking place in one country being recorded and accounted for in a company in another country is not new for the era of Amazon, Google, Apple, and similar companies. More than thirty-five years ago, this concept was identified and developed by shipping companies.

Traditionally, shipping companies appointed agents who billed customers, accounted for the revenues and costs, and eventually remitted the net proceeds to the shipping line. This system had the major disadvantage that large sums of money sat in agents' bank accounts for long periods. The solution to this problem lay in two facts. The commercial transaction between the customer and the shipping line was agreed in a point-to-point bill of lading whereby for a fee the shipping line transported, for example, a container from Birmingham, Great Britain to Beijing. The agent only acted on behalf of the company and was not party to the commercial contract. Secondly, one of the most under-rated developments in 'globalisation' occurred: the widespread use by companies of a powerful accounting software developed by, amongst others, SAP in Germany, allowing transactions to be created, stored and filed (accounted for) anywhere in the world between group (and other) companies.

The leap was made: bill the customer, collect the money, pay necessary costs locally, but record all the relevant transactions in the shipping company's books in its country of incorporation. Combine this with a daily cash-clearing facility to a central treasury (that is collect all the cash into one central bank account in the home country), and total transparency and control is achieved. This development coincided with the reduction in the use of third-party agents and the setting-up of wholly owned subsidiary companies in most countries. It was not lost on shipping companies that one other advantage of this system was that subsidiary companies could then be operated on a cost-plus basis either directly, where allowed, or through a volume-related remuneration agreement which resulted in a small operating profit sufficient to ensure that the company was solvent and seen to pay some tax.

This arrangement can be justified because the contracted service, the bill of lading, is an international, legally recognised, service on the high seas provided by the shipping company using their assets, the ship. For shipping companies and for individual countries, this system makes sense. The commercial agreement is an end-to-end price, the element assigned to the inland and loading/discharge cost may or may not be cost-covering. The profit or loss for the shipping company will be on the total revenue less total cost.

In the legal framework of international shipping, this concept is justified. Can it be justified in the context of a company shipping a book by post from Bochum, Germany, to Birmingham, Great Britain?

Before trying to answer this question, it is necessary to briefly describe the legal base of a bill of lading. The law surrounding this is long-standing and extremely complex but at its simplest, the bill of lading is evidence that a contract of carriage exists between the shipper and the shipping company and usually sets out the terms of the contract.

"The bill of lading is a legally binding document that provides the carrier and shipper with all of the necessary details to accurately process a shipment. It has three main functions. First, it is a document of title to the goods described in the bill of lading. Secondly, it is a receipt for the shipped products. Finally, the bill of lading represents the agreed terms and conditions for the transportation of the goods."[75]

---

[75] Investopedia.

It is also important to add that a bill of lading is a negotiable document of title.

The contention, therefore, that the owner of valuable goods handing them over under contract to a shipping company under a negotiable document is somewhat different from Mr Smith ordering a book from Amazon in Birmingham, Great Britain to be delivered by post from Germany, for example, is not stretching the comparison too far. How can it be that these two cases can be treated in Britain in a similar way?

The short answer is that they should not be, and that there are many possible reasons why the government does not exercise the powers at its disposal. A review of the filed accounts of Amazon companies in Britain shows that, whilst in 1998 the Amazon UK company recorded all transactions through its books, during 1999 it moved the recording of sales and purchase transactions abroad and left the British company as a cost centre: that is, sufficient income was put into it to ensure it did not make a loss.

The financial statements show all this and give the details of 'discontinued operations' but make no comment on the major change this represents, nor do they show where the transactions went, nor any indication of the rationale behind it. It is to be assumed that this major change was cleared with the Inland Revenue (now HMRC) as without doubt the Inland Revenue must wish to be able to collect VAT and, since the sales were in Britain, corporation tax on any profits generated in Britain.

There is also no indication in the financial statements of how the turnover of the company is calculated. As a cost-plus operation, it must be assumed that after finalising all costs, charges were made to the immediate parent company in Luxembourg, although in 2000 not sufficient to avoid a loss of £154,998. One wonders what the reaction, if any, of the Inland Revenue was to this move, which appears to be simply designed to move taxable revenue and costs offshore.

The auditors were now also clear that the company was trading only with its parent company and that without that support it was not viable. Note 1 on accounting policies makes this clear: "The accounts have been prepared on the going concern basis as the parent undertaking has agreed to provide continuing financial support to allow the company to meet its obligations as they fall due." Clearly, the auditors had insisted on a letter of comfort, otherwise they would qualify the accounts.

At this point it is unclear how the Inland Revenue was fulfilling its duty to collect VAT and corporation tax, but one must assume that it was.

The British Government must have woken up to the fact that control and transparency in respect of businesses transferring taxable activity in Britain abroad was insufficient and passed the Overseas Companies Regulation 2009. This rather grand name did not place particularly onerous requirements on a foreign company trading in Britain but effectively only required it to file its own accounts and give some basic details. There was, surprisingly, no requirement to show the business activity relating to the British business, nor any requirements for specific details of transactions to be available, or for access to this detail by the Inland Revenue. This exacting requirement meant filling in a simple form and filing the parent company accounts.

For some inexplicable reason, the first filed form from Amazon EU Sarl, the parent company, was filed in 2015, six years after the passing of the Act. As always when examining British company law and its application, one assumes that there are rational explanations for these facts, but transparency is not there.

So, unlike the long-standing legal convention surrounding international shipping, a large retailer can emulate the structure with the minimum of transparency for the citizen but not, one hopes, for the government and Inland Revenue.

One of the major obstacles to formulating a straightforward proposal to simplify treatment of recording the activity and taxing such companies is the view that as 'tech' companies they are somehow qualitatively different from other companies. They are different from international shipping companies but not different from any other retailing and service companies which sell cross-border. The major shipping companies invested, far earlier than the 'tech' companies, huge amounts in IT which enabled them, using massive relational databases, to record every small aspect of their business worldwide, and to cost in detail every one of millions of moves everywhere in the world. They were by this definition early 'tech' companies but are not identified as such. Amazon and similar companies use the same technology for retailing and service provision.

What is different is that identifying the profit element in simple retail and service provision is not impossible. It should not even be difficult. Every item must be billed to the customer in the country where the service is provided, in Britain for VAT purposes, so turnover is clear. Cost is the bought-in price of an item, although transfer pricing must be audited to ensure no irregular profit transfer takes place. One challenging area is the allocation of overheads, particularly IT costs, but this can be calculated proportionally from the parent company financial statements after ignoring all incoming intercompany charges for royalties and licences. From the point of view of the tax authorities this is precisely the area in which they should be interested as if profits are being moved between countries it will either be here or in transfer pricing. That is a different and local calculation. There are, no doubt, sections of HMRC tasked with reviewing all these companies but evidence available does not enable us to assess their skill or effectiveness.

It is not unreasonable to expect that a government, wishing to collect taxes due from companies and individuals, would require companies to accurately record their commercial transactions in local currency and in conformity with local legal and accounting requirements in the country where they took place. India is an example of a country which does this. This would give a reliable overview and make any audit easier and more transparent. Countries have this power, but for whatever reason choose, nearly always, not to use it. The avoidance and evasion of tax by multinational companies is not unknown. I deliberately use the word 'evasion' since transfer pricing abuses are illegal and are widely used. The fact that most tax authorities are either under-resourced or, as a matter of policy, do not generally pursue this abuse means that it is greatly under-taxed. Despite having nine current live investigations (January 2024), and despite the Corporate Criminal Offence coming into force in 2017, there has not been a prosecution of a company by HMRC.

A company cannot commit an offence; doing so requires the active participation of one or more human actors and if it can be shown that a company has deliberately broken tax law and committed an offence, any penalty should involve the senior management; either the directors or, if identifiable, the senior management who deliberately broke the company's internal regulations on tax conformity, as is the case in a number of other countries.

This would be widely seen as just (returning to Rawls and the concept of justice) as "Our analysis of government criminal justice system statistics reveals that in the 11 years to 2019: 23 times as many people are prosecuted for benefits related offences as they are for tax related offences. Over the 11-year period 13,540 people were handed suspended or immediate custodial sentences for benefits related offences, compared with 1,601 people for tax related offences. This despite the fact that DWP categorise £2.2bn as arising from fraud, accounting for 1.2% of the total benefits bill whilst the total gross tax gap attributable to fraud at £20bn ... will be a significant underestimate, because HMRC's tax gap does not include significant areas of avoidance such as profit shifting by multinational companies which means that the real tax gap is significantly higher."[76] It should be pointed out again here that deliberately overpricing internal transfers is evasion and not avoidance! This whole area of multinational company tax avoidance and evasion is widely measured and reported; the excellent Nicholas Shaxson (Treasure Island, The Finance Curse), Tax Watch and Tax Justice Network (see Bibliography) regularly analyse and quantify the problem.

It is important to remember that the government collects the taxes due to be paid under the law on behalf of all citizens. All citizens and businesses would wish for confirmation that in the same way they correctly pay their tax liability, all others are equally obliged to meet the same obligation. In 2022/23 HMRC lost an estimated £836 million from 'phoenixing', where companies are repeatedly liquidated and set up under new names. This is tax evasion, which is illegal. This amount, however, is likely to be significantly underestimated according to the House of Commons public accounts committee in February 2025.

When using the power of the state to oblige citizens to meet their tax obligations, it is essential that this requirement is enforced equally and transparently by officers of the state with the power to use the legal authority of the state to ensure compliance. It is extremely worrying when HMRC

---

[76] Tax Watch, Equality Before the Law.

addresses taxpayers as 'customer', it sends the wrong message and raises the question as to whether HMRC has been given the correct instruction. It would be helpful if serious breaches of tax law which constituted a felony, with sanctions available including imprisonment, were applied with greater vigour.

The purpose of this short excursion through this subject and look at one company (there are many more even bigger examples) is to re-enforce the point that for all multi-national companies all politics is local/national. We have already noted that the multi-national holding company heads, usually, a vast number of individual companies all responsible to a particular country legally and for tax purposes. There is no overarching body (the European Union is an exception, but on a limited scale); even an international agreement by, for example, the OECD, which is extremely unlikely, would have to be enacted in detail in legislation by each individual country to which it was intended to apply.

Justice and fairness demand that a country's tax authority, operated by the government on behalf of all its citizens, should not only operate neutrally and fairly but should be seen to operate in this way. A citizen's tax affairs, provided they are correctly carried out are, quite rightly, private. The tax affairs of major companies and multi-national companies are subject to publication as part of the annual financial statement but there are now large gaps in this transparency where the United Kingdom tax authorities make private, i.e. non-public, agreements with major companies.

The Global Perspective

Chapter 15
China

We have seen that the existing, multilateral organisations overseeing corporate activity worldwide are breaking down and that the prospect of a worldwide control over corporate activity, as proposed by and supported by many commentators, is receding. As this trend continues, the only effective way for governments to exercise control over such companies is by assuming control themselves through the obvious route of company law, developed for and with the citizens of the country. In the absence of multilateral efforts this is necessary, but what resistance is a country such as Britain likely to face internationally, should it choose to follow this course? Challenges and attempts to derail it would come from powerful countries who, for whatever reason, would believe that such changes were not in their interest or, better expressed, not in the interest of their own companies.

What countries, or groupings of countries, if they wished to be obstructive, would be powerful enough to try to derail the efforts of another sovereign country? On the assumption that we are not contemplating military action, only the United States, the European Union, China, and in the future possibly India would fall into this category. By looking into the corporate and political structures and connections within these countries, it should be possible to show the likelihood of both the attempt, and any likely success.

Let's begin with China.

Is a totalitarian capitalist state always a fascist state? A state controlling all aspects of a citizen's life headed by an unelected, self-perpetuating oligarchy? We have viewed China as a communist totalitarian state following Maoist principles of collective ownership but for many years now it has been moving strongly in a capitalist direction, with companies, company and mercantile law, stock exchanges, and an expanding class of private owners. At this speed, how long before China becomes the world's largest and most powerful capitalist state?

This should give us pause for thought, as it opens a new possible direction for world politics to take. As a communist, closed-off country, China was a military threat assumed to be anxious to transpose its system all over the world. Now it is part of the world capitalist system; a member of the WTO with subsidiaries of major companies from all countries doing business within its borders. Doing business today in China as a foreign-owned company is similar to doing business in 1930s Germany. There is codified law to follow and provided this is adhered to, and that no overtly political activity (except that approved by the state) is carried out, and the authorities are kept informed, business goes on satisfactorily.

There are other advantages. Money and effort spent cultivating political leaders is usually unlikely to be wasted by their being voted out of office. Equally, with no free press (or free anything), there is little oversight of activity and especially no troublesome non-state unions, or health and safety or environmental questions to be answered.

What does this mean for the future of democracy?

Major US companies, as we will see, have achieved a situation where both political parties capable of being elected are funded substantially by them or their supporters and where the political agenda and law-making can be steered to their needs. Democracy does not, therefore, represent any threat to their pre-eminent position or control of the political agenda. This is the ideal position for the corporation to achieve, to have the cover of democracy but through the power of subsidy prevent undesirable change or risk to profits, and therefore to salary and bonus levels, and to control over levels of taxation.

The situation in China is potentially more dangerous to the management of companies as the oligarchy does not need the financial subsidy to be elected and therefore is not in the power of the senior management of the corporations. If we take a crystal ball and look into the future, how may China appear? The best prototype may be today's Singapore. A capitalist country: a haven for major world companies, respected by senior corporate leaders for its strong, business-friendly government, but tightly controlled politically.

China is ostensibly not a capitalist country but a communist one. Its forays into capitalism are recent. Following the assumption of control by Deng Xiaoping in 1976, and the subsequent pursuit of economic growth a Sino-foreign joint venture, law was introduced to legalise the formation of foreign-invested limited liability companies.

The next major step was the introduction of a unified company law in 1993. It was revised in 1999 and 2003 and effectively completely re-written in 2005. This 2005 version is therefore usually referred to as the new 2005 Company Law. It is worth looking at the nature of Chinese company law to understand how the Chinese government and business may view company law in other jurisdictions.

"It is increasingly difficult to characterise China's evolving legal system as belonging to either the civil law or common law family... although China has extensively borrowed legal concepts, principles, terminologies, institutions and procedures from Anglo-American jurisdictions (most significantly the United States), it remains a civilian jurisdiction at least insofar as sources of law are concerned."[77]

Further, although China's corporate law embraces a significant number of institutions imported from foreign sources, it is difficult to identify the single most significant 'origin' country. "Broadly speaking, the Chinese system is a hybrid one, having institutions borrowed from both the common law family, mainly the United States, and continental civil law family, i.e. Germany."[78]

In examining where Chinese company law differs from British company law, it is worth looking in detail at certain Articles. Perhaps the most obvious difference is Article 19.

"An organisation of the Communist Party of China (CPC) shall be established in a company to carry out party activities according to the Charter of the Communist Party of China. The company shall provide necessary conditions for the activities of the organisation of the CPC."

A cynic may wish to argue that any further examination of the law would be pointless, but this is not the case. There are a number of articles in China's company law which indicate that the country may not wish, or be able, to challenge the proposed changes to British company law. Two connected articles are of interest.

Article 5 states: "A company shall, when engaging in business activities, abide by laws and administrative regulations, observe social moralities and business ethics, act in good faith, accept the supervision of the Government and the public, and undertake social responsibilities. The legitimate rights and interests of a company shall be protected by law and shall not be infringed upon."

This article can be linked to Article 147 on the duty of directors, which states: "The directors, supervisors and senior management personnel of a company shall abide by

---

[77] Company Law in China, Jiangyu Wang, Edward Elgar, 2014.
[78] Ibid.

laws, administrative regulations and the company's Articles of Association and have a duty of loyalty and a duty of care to the company."

Professor Wang correctly draws attention to the difference between Article 147 and the broadly drawn standards set for directors in British company law to 'promote the success of the company' with requirements for 'good faith' but no actual requirement to follow the law of the land, and no penalties for not doing so.

There are two basic company forms under Chinese company law: the Limited Liability Company (LLC) and the Joint-stock Limited Company (JSLC). The LLC can be compared to the US closely held corporation and the 'private company' in English common law jurisdictions. One major difference is that the LLC does not issue shares, but the shareholder's capital is defined by the percentage of capital injected. Company law also allows the forming of a one-person limited liability company but with the proviso of Article 63: "Where the shareholder of a one-person limited liability company is unable to prove that the property of the company is independent of his/her own property, the shareholder shall bear joint and several liabilities for the debts of the company."

This particular Article carries a sting in the tail as a commentary by the NPC Legislative Affairs Commission states: "a company 100 percent owned by another company is both a subsidiary and a one-person company, and as such must comply with the provisions of [the Company Law] concerning a one person company."[79]

There is therefore a 'presumption of guilt' in terms of limited liability.

Although not stipulated in company law, legal opinion in China suggests that the corporate veil could be pierced by

---

[79] Ibid.

under-capitalisation, either initially or by draining capital, by using the company as a device for avoiding contractual obligations, to evade statutory restrictions or by confusion of private and company affairs. China would therefore have some sympathy with a proposal to remove limited liability from subsidiary companies.

To form an LLC, RMB30,000 (£ 3,300) is needed and for a JSLC, RMB 5 million (£550,000); much larger than the minimal amounts needed in the United Kingdom. It is also necessary to note that the capital needed to form a Foreign Invested Company is extremely high and will be a percentage of the proposed investment but in any event, unlike in Britain, will be many millions of pounds. With a nod towards German company law, a company must set up a 'statutory common reserve fund' and allocate 10% of its after-tax profits, up to a level of 50% of its registered capital, if it decides to make a distribution in a given year. Premiums earned on the issuance of shares at above par go into a common reserve fund, which may not be used for making up the company's losses.

Having moved from a broadly agricultural economy to the appearance of a relatively sophisticated capitalist economy in less than a generation, has China really changed radically? Informed commentators, both foreign and national, believe not; nor is it realistically to be expected.

"At the start of the 1990s, all Chinese companies had been unformed state-owned enterprises; by the end of the decade, hundreds were listed companies on the Hong Kong, New York, London and Shanghai stock exchanges. In those few short years, bankers, lawyers and accountants had restructured those of the old SOEs (state owned companies) that could be restructured into something resembling modern corporations, then sold and listed their shares. In short, China's Fortune Global 500 companies were the product of Wall Street... The state-owned National Champions dominate the domestic economy whilst the foreign and non-state sectors are the drivers of the export boom and will be supported as long as they are critical as a source of jobs."[80]

Few query the power of the nomenklatura list whose members find themselves in both senior political and business positions, along with their families, relations and retainers. Controlling all this activity is the CSRC [China Securities Regulatory Commission] with the state being involved at every stage of the market as the regulator, the policy maker, the investor, the parent company, the listed company, and the banker. So, no meaningful opening to foreign participation can be expected. It is always helpful to highlight the way business is done in China.

"Anbang (a Chinese company) is a case in point. The group company... Has never published an audited financial statement. Neither does it divulge the identity of its ultimate owners, ... The company's enigmatic chairman, Wu Xiaohui, 49, is thought to enjoy strong connections within the Communist Party elite, partly through his marriage to the granddaughter of Deng Xiaoping, the architect of modern China."[81]

But in China high-level connections do not always provide protection. "Wu Xiaohui, founder of Anbang Insurance, is facing personal as well as corporate scrutiny. Known for his high-flying lifestyle and audacious takeover bids, Mr Wu was detained by authorities earlier this month."[82]

---

[80] Red Capitalism, Walter Howie, Wiley, 2012.

[81] Anbang Insurance Group Co Ltd China Inc: The quest for cash flow
The Big Read MARCH 18, 2016 by: James Kynge, Gabriel Wildau and Don Weinland
https://www.ft.com/content/020b064c-ecfe-11e5-bb79-2303682345c8)

[82] Dalian Wanda Group Co Ltd
China probe shines light on top dealmakers

It can be dangerous for businessmen to fly too near to the sun.

"The crackdown on the private sector kicked off in June with the midnight detention of Wu Xiaohui ... Mr Wu has not been heard from since... The seemingly technical issue of a drop in foreign exchange reserves has become a political weapon as President Xi Jinping tries to consolidate enough power to control his own succession."[83]

Under these circumstances is it not reasonable to expect that China will wish to assert it economic power against a country looking to strengthen its company law in favour of the state and the citizen? Experience suggests not; despite the continuing power politics within China, in the economic sphere Chinese actions over the last few decades have been the antithesis of this. During its long-negotiated accession to and membership of the World Trade Organization, China maintained a quiet, careful position, and continues to do so. When it was suggested that China assert itself, Chinese negotiators responded: "China is not a leader and China does not want to be a leader." A negotiator explained: "We would have to take the spotlight and that is against China's philosophy to be quiet, low profile, modest."

Such a strategy is in keeping with Deng Xiaoping's famous directive of taoguang yanghui, that the country should "observe developments soberly, maintain our position, meet challenges calmly, hide our capabilities and bide our time, remain free from ambition and never claim leadership."

Perhaps the most telling phrase in the final quotation is 'hide our capabilities and bide our time'. In recent years,

JUNE 22, 2017 by: Arash Massoudi and Lucy Hornby
https://www.ft.com/content/ba7fc7b4-575e-11e7-9fed-c19e2700005f)
[83] (The Big Read China Business & Finance
Chinese crackdown on dealmakers reflects Xi power play. Lucy Hornby
https://www.ft.com/content/ed900da6-769b-11e7-90c0-90a9d1bc9691

China has invested heavily throughout the world. Over the past two decades, China has increased trade with Latin American and Caribbean countries 26-fold, from $12bn to $310bn, surpassing trade between the region and the EU and making China their second-largest trading partner, behind the US. This has placed China in competition with the European Union, which is also anxious to expand trade with this region.

At a Latin America and Caribbean/European Union summit, Columbia's president said, "There's a greater social conscience in the European Union compared to North American society, which also has a denialist tendency in the climate crisis. But China's vast funding makes it a more attractive partner because China has a greater planning power than the European Union."[84]

Earlier we saw that, according to the European Union, Ineos was in a 50/50 partnership with Petro-China, which reflected a deliberate and targeted move by Chinese companies into major European companies and assets. There is evidence that the extent of this move and the underlying risks of state or party control over Chinese companies is causing some concern in Europe. Invoking national security concerns, Italy has stripped China's Sinochem, which owns a 37% stake in the business, of its influence as the largest shareholder in Pirelli, removing its right to appoint the CEO or set the tyre-maker's strategy. Sinochem, which owns its stake through China National Rubber Company, will also be barred from involvement in decisions about Pirelli's mergers and acquisitions, sales, spin-offs or listings of financial instruments.[85] It has also

[84] FT@newsletters.ft.com on behalf of Henry Foy <FT@newsletters.ft.com>
Sent: 18 July 2023 06:00
Europe Express: Choosing China over EU.)
[85] Italy Strips China's Sinochem of its influence as Pirelli's largest investor

told Pirelli to refuse any requests from China's state-owned Assets Supervision and Administration Commission of the State Council, including for information-sharing. The two companies will also have to keep their treasury and cash-pooling functions separate.

As well as being a move to limit the power of a Chinese company over a national asset, this has illustrated how countries, should they so wish, can intervene to protect key assets. The Italian move is mirrored by moves by the United States Government to ban US investment in some of China's tech industries. The reality, however, is that such actions are and will probably remain limited. "An analysis of financial data by Nikkei Asia shows that of the top 100 global companies in China by sales in the most recent fiscal year, 17 were US tech-related companies."[86]

Nothing suggests that China, the Middle Kingdom, would take any steps to counter changes in British company law which would, in many respects, move it closer to the Chinese model.

In examining Britain's relationship with the EU, I emphasised the different experiences during and after the Second World War in creating its view of the EU and attitudes towards it. A similar approach is necessary when considering China and Britain; taking the period 1912 to 1989 Britain was not invaded and was, internally, peaceful. From the setting up of the Republic of China on 1st January 1912, which overthrew the Manchu-led Qing dynasty and

Amy Kazmin in Rome and Sylvia Sciorilli Borrelli in Milan
Milan June 18 2023
https://www.ft.com/content/1cc91834-ef81-4a5d-9efd-edc5146ba1a3
[86] Asian tech can't quit China and Netflix dives into Asia
Akito Tanaka, Grave Li, Qianer Liu, Tomoko Wagasuki, Shunsuki Tabeta, Rei Nakafuji and Kotaro Hosokawa, July 13 2023.
https://www.ft.com/content/d69554c0-0252-4ef1-81a4-c3699ead4a54

ended China's imperial history, to 1927, when the Kuomintang reunified the country, until 1949 after their defeat in the Chinese Civil War, China experienced only violence. It has been estimated that between 1.8 million and 3.5 million people died between 1927 and 1949, including deaths from forced conscription and massacres.

In 1931, the Japanese invaded Manchuria, followed by a series of smaller encroachments and ultimately a full-scale invasion of China in 1937. The Second World War devastated China, leading to enormous loss of life and material destruction. War with Japan continued until its surrender in September 1945.

The post-1945 history of China was equally turbulent, with social chaos and considerable loss of life during the Cultural Revolution up until the 1989 Tiananmen Square massacre. More recent history has brought a period of relative stability; it is likely that the Chinese leadership wishes to concentrate on improving conditions within China to maintain that stability within a country of 1.4 billion people rather than embark on outside adventures, particularly over the issue of company law.

Chapter 16
European Union

As Britain has now left the European Union and is no longer a signatory to the Treaties, neither is it directly bound by the Directives and Treaties of the Union.

The effect of European Union membership on United Kingdom company law is covered in Chapter 11, and it is still to be seen how far, if at all, these changes are kept or reversed. Here, we are concerned with the reaction of the European Union member states to the proposed changes in United Kingdom company law set out in this book. I think it is reasonable to state that this reaction is unlikely to be obstructive. Firstly, as noted previously, there is no codified European company law as such and member states continue to operate separate company acts, which are amended from time to time to comply with EU directives and regulations. The European Union has also demonstrated by, for example, its action against Ireland for offering lower corporation tax rates to foreign companies than to its own companies, that it is against a 'race to the bottom' in respect of corporate tax rates. Equally, the social market principles of the Union are predicated on a reasonable tax income on the part of member countries. There is no reason to suppose that the proposed changes would not be viewed neutrally by the Union as presenting no threat to the union model and by preventing Britain itself entering a corporate 'race to the bottom' in respect of regulation and tax levels. Equally, the question of a referral to the European Court of Justice should a company believe that its rights, including human rights (a contradiction in terms), have been breached is removed.

A more interesting question is whether, on studying the suggested changes, the European Union might be brought to follow some or all of the proposals. There is every reason to hope that this may be the case in direct contra-distinction to China and to the United States. The reason for this optimism is that the European Union is premised on a belief in the citizen, and that his or her wellbeing is the key purpose and the driving force behind the long road towards European unity set out in the Treaties creating the Union.

The European Union places the citizen at the centre of its political and economic objectives but the traditional dilemma is unavoidable: how do you prioritise the objectives, and who decides? Perhaps more importantly, what principles do you employ in making these decisions? Because of the nature of the Treaties and the participation of many countries, the European Union has to rely to a great degree on the market and market forces but, as we saw when looking at China, this is a disadvantage when competing with a country which also employs state planning and control. It may be necessary, when looking at the climate crisis and the need to urgently decarbonise the economy, at 'planning' at the state or European Union level, and in doing so to weigh the needs of the most disadvantaged citizen against the demands of powerful companies.

The principles set out in Rawls' A Theory of Justice are usable but do require judgement on the part of the user. This cannot, however, be a convincing objection as the same argument must apply to any attempted use of utilitarian theory of the greatest good of the greatest number. I find Rawls' theory the less difficult to apply.

The greatest good of the greatest number requires overarching judgements over great swathes of the political economy and its economic units. When applying 'principles of justice', one needs to consider what a group of informed citizens would decide when faced with a specific decision such as, for example, the role of a company director, or the correct and fair level of a minimum wage, or what legal requirements can be placed on a company to speed up and enable decarbonisation to proceed, whilst being unaware of their own position in society. Not easy, but infinitely easier than the 'grand scheme' approach. It should still be possible to conduct such conceptualising within the European Union, and I would like to think that it might still be possible in Britain.

In this context, the success of the European Union is of profound importance as it remains one of the few substantial beacons in the world dedicated to a democratic future for an important group of countries. The role Britain played in setting up the precursor to the European Union is often overlooked, as is the split over the organisation's future in the 1950s; a harbinger of the deep divisions in Britain in respect of membership of the European Union. The nature of the relationship between the EU and Britain can best be seen by considering briefly its relationship with one of the founding organisations of the EU.

The beginnings of the European Movement coincided with the end of the Second World War. No surprise there, but there is always a danger of reading history backwards. The success and stability that we see today in a broadly united Europe were not inevitable, nor was the success of the European Movement certain. There was no cause for optimism in 1945.

European civilisation was on its knees; the geo-political picture was apocalyptic. Fighting ended in 1945 but the reprisals, expulsions by the million, and the search for lost relatives and general chaos went on for years afterwards. Countries that had never been, had scarcely been, or had been, democracies were all searching for a democratic future. Eastern Europe was falling under the grip of the USSR and Spain and Portugal were fascist dictatorships (to remain so until the mid-1970s). Those countries of Europe actively seeking security were small in number!

Surveying this grim outlook, most democratic politicians who had survived the war saw some unification of Europe as essential to prevent a future descent into chaos. The details of the foundation of the European Movement are well known, and I will only touch on them here.

The International Committee of the Movements for European Union, founded in November 1947 and chaired by Briton Duncan Sandys, convened and hosted the Congress of Europe in the Hague in May 1948 with Winston Churchill as its honorary president, and with over 800 delegates. The Congress agreed on the ambitious task of promoting European unity. It soon became apparent that this enormous task could not be left in the hands of the many activist associations and in Brussels in October 1948 the ICMEU changed its name to the European Movement and elected as its presidents former French Prime Minister Leon Blum, Winston Churchill, Italian Prime Minister Alcide de Gaspari and the Belgian Prime Minister and Foreign Minister Paul-Henri Spaak. These were very swiftly followed by the French Foreign Minister, Robert Schuman, Count Richard Coudenhove-Kalergi, and the German Chancellor, Konrad Adenauer.

As one of its early major achievements, the Statute of the Council of Europe – a somewhat toned-down version of the proposals and recommendations of the European Movement – was signed in London on May 5th 1949, setting up the Council of Europe.

In April 1949, the European Movement held an economic conference in London at which, not for the last time, differences emerged between the British delegation which supported sovereignty and the formation of a free trade area and a significant number of continental European delegates who favoured a partial surrender of sovereignty and an economic and customs union.

British resistance increased in late 1949 and early 1950 as Sandys and Churchill sensed that the European Movement was moving much faster than the British Conservative Party and establishment wished. By early 1950, the European Movement was in some difficulty. The Movement was torn between its British and Continental European leadership, leading to considerable discord. The Chair of the American Committee for a United Europe, which was providing substantial funds to the Movement, visited Europe and backed the vision of the continental Europeans. In July 1950, Sandys resigned as Chairman, to be replaced by Spaak, and the European integrationists took control. At the same time, the International Secretariat of the European Movement was moved from London to Brussels.

This was a decisive moment in the history of the European Movement and of Europe as it set the direction for the next fifty years of development in European politics and led directly to the united Europe we have today.

Despite this development, the role which Churchill played in both setting up and securing the financing of the European Movement and the role the Movement played in setting Europe on the road to unity cannot be exaggerated.

Europe was not only damaged but it was also bankrupt, and only the United States had the funds to finance development. We therefore need also to cover an important but little-known part of the history of the European Movement. In the summer of 1948, a small delegation from the European Movement (including Sandys) arrived in the United States to urge the formation of an American committee to support their own efforts for unification. A new body, the American Committee on United Europe, was formed to support Churchill and the European Movement. The Chair was General William Donovan, head of the OSS in London during the war and a friend of Churchill's. Other senior members were mainly military and intelligence people, also largely from London. As these men subsequently and logically also became senior intelligence figures in the US government, there is a tendency to see the committee as a US intelligence invention. Again, this is to read history backwards: they were old friends of Churchill. In March 1949, Churchill visited New York to discuss final details with Donovan and Dulles and to attend the formal launch of ACUE, which took the form of a public lunch in his honour.

Churchill, at once the most prominent advocate of European unity and the best-known transatlantic evangelist, was the vital link between the ACUE and the European Movement. He enjoyed unrivalled personal contacts with American and European leaders, and he shared the view of Donovan and Dulles that the promotion of European unity through ACUE was the unofficial counterpart to the Marshall Plan. Between 1949 and 1960, when it was disbanded, the ACUE injected over $3 million from private individuals and foundations into the European Movement and provided between a half and two thirds of its budget. There is no evidence that the ACUE attempted to manipulate organisations or individuals; it sought genuinely independent vehicles that seemed complementary to American policy and tried to speed them up. The history of the ACUE shows us prominent European politicians in search of discrete American aid, rather than the CIA in search of proxies.

In the spring of 1951, under Spaak's new leadership, the European Movement was an effective organisation pushing to create support for the Schuman Plan and for more authority for the Council of Europe and for a European army. Between 1951 and 1956, the European Movement organised over 2000 rallies and festivals on the Continent.

On the continent of Europe, the Movement was influential and well-funded, being in tune with the direction of travel of most governments.

Turning to the European Movement in the UK after 1950, there are two very distinct periods to consider; the early 1950s to the 1980s, and the period after this. Britain and the British Government's attitude to European integration can be seen in the position of the British press over the last fifty years. The perennial question as to whether the press (or its owners) influenced the government or reflected the government position is too big to discuss here.

Between 1948 and 1975 (the year of the first referendum on membership of the then European Economic Community), the British press moved from a vaguely pro-community consensus to a pronounced and nearly unanimous Euro-enthusiasm. The media took a considerable time to realise the significance of Britain's exclusion from the European Economic Community; not until the collapse of the Free Trade Area negotiations in 1958 did the bulk of the press begin to question the wisdom of the government's European policy. The press, which was overwhelmingly supportive of the Conservatives, tended to reinforce that party's belief in the economic benefits of membership.

When did the change in attitudes towards European integration begin? Probably in the later 1980s, around the time that Commission President Jacques Delors articulated a vision of closer union and mutual co-operation followed by Margaret Thatcher's sceptical speech in Bruges arguing that the community should be nothing more than a partnership of trading states. Here we were, back again to 1951 and the early divergence between continental Europe and Britain.

How is this reflected in the history of the European Movements in Britain? Starting in 1963-64, the Conservative Government made grants to the European

Movement UK; in 1969 it was £7,500, about a third of its total income. Bear in mind that in 1969 you could buy a nice house in London for that amount. The anti-EEC group in Parliament targeted the European Movement because it was the only substantial pro-European integration organisation at that time. The peak of European Movement influence in Britain certainly occurred in 1975 when, under the umbrella 'Britain in Europe', the Movement took the lead in supporting the 'in' campaign and was in turn supported by the government. This relationship continued to some extent through the 1980s so that in October 1988 the responsible minister, Linda Chalker, could state in Parliament, "The European Movement has a valuable role to play in drawing public attention and that of businessmen and women and industry to the advantages of completion of the single market." Once again, the apparently transactional nature of the government's relations with both the then EEC and the European Movement UK is worth noting!

In 1992, the Foreign and Commonwealth Office made a grant of £30,000 to the European Movement UK to fund regional conferences on the Maastricht Treaty, after which overt support effectively ceased, marking the end of the relationship between British governments and the European Movement as the political climate in respect of European integration began to change. The European Movement UK continued to campaign tirelessly for European integration, despite the fact that all subsequent governments appear to have adopted a position which at best could be summarised as Europe will always remain an external 'other'; an image against which British identity can be defined and projected. Britain's presence in an integrated Europe was and is always presented as transactional, with no ideological or principled underpinning, despite the fact that successive governments appeared to be committed to remaining members of the European Union. Whilst wishing to remain in the EU, they were terrified of raising the spectre of Euroscepticism. Unlike in Continental Europe, no British government in the future was anxious to be seen to be associated with an organisation so committed to European integration for the benefit of its citizens.

Its failure could well lead to the eventual ending of democracy as a political fact. Much of the political economic writing in the mid- and late-20th century was produced in the United States by Europeans horrified by the failures of that continent as a result of totalitarian ideologies of both left and right. For them, the state was the enemy and should be kept as small as possible. This line of thought dominated the later 20th century and was eagerly adopted by financial interests, particularly in the United States, to justify the effective obliteration of all state activity except basic legal functions and law and order... This morbid pessimism on the role of the state should be rejected but can only be defended if there are clear ways of ensuring that the democratic state exists to aid and protect its citizens. The European Union should guarantee this.

Within such a supra-national organisation, the role of the company can be discussed and set out for the benefit of all citizens within the concept of Rawls' 'justice' without injuring either the wealthy entrepreneur or the poorest citizen. The poison of the 20th century dichotomy of capitalism against socialism, where only one can win, has distorted the discussion of political economy for too long. By structuring company law correctly, everyone benefits; only the dishonest are disadvantaged, and they will never be happy, but the neutral, informed citizen will see that their interests are best served wherever they might fit into the social structure. One needs to go further and say that presently only company law can achieve this as internationally there are no structures to defend the citizen from excessive exploitation.

Chapter 17
The US

The very scale and complexity of US company law and its role in US life and politics is so extensive that it is worth restating at the outset the question to be answered here. Should Britain radically redraw its company laws, both as a response to a lack of global control over companies and as a matter of principle to protect and improve the lives of its citizens, would the US follow that example, or challenge those changes, passively or aggressively?

On the face of it, Britain and the United States have a shared history of company law, both being common law countries with an emphasis on judge-made case law. The situation in the United States is complicated by the federal nature of United States politics and the extensive powers resting with individual states. As well as a Federal Constitution, with a Supreme Court and legislature, each state has its own version of these.

Company law, with certain exceptions, is within the competence of the states and, at least in theory, the states all have their own company laws. Under the concept of 'implied powers', the Federal Government takes to itself powers not specifically defined in the Constitution: in this context, the most important of these is the power over interstate commerce. This power is defined by the Supreme Court. We will see the relevance of this later.

With company law powers lying with the states, the Federal Government limits itself to regulating for "minimum standards for trade in company shares and governance rights such as the Security and Exchange Act of

1934 or the Sarbanes-Oxley Act of 2002."[87]

Widely adopted throughout the United States is the American Bar Association Revised Model Business Corporation Act, which is not mandatory, and certain states maintain their own rules.

One state dominates the United States company incorporation scene. A half of all publicly traded corporations in the United States are incorporated in the State of Delaware, which does not follow the Revised Model Business Corporation Act and is generally seen to be pro-business.

The importance of the implied power over interstate commerce becomes clearer when it is seen that the Privileges and Immunities Clause (Article XIV United States Constitution), which protects fundamental rights of US citizens from being infringed upon by state governments, ensuring that states cannot deny citizens of their federal rights, is not applicable to companies.

"According to the case law of the US Supreme Court it rejects the concept of a corporate citizen and states that corporations 'are creatures of local law and have not even an absolute right of recognition in other states, but depend for that and for the enforcement of their contracts upon the assent of those states, which may be given accordingly on such terms as they please'."[88]

There are two sides to the Interstate Commerce Clause: whilst it prohibits Congress from legislating on commerce within the states, it also prohibits states from imposing regulatory burdens on interstate commerce. The scope of the second part is still contested but is viewed as limiting the

---

[87] Dauphine University Paris, Comparative Corporate Law, the US corporation and the French SA. Thesis, Hugo Kerbib 2107.
[88] William and Mary Business law Review. Volume 4, Issue 1, Article 1. Company Law in the European Union and the United States. Christoph Allmendinger. 2013.

ability of state law to discriminate against corporations incorporated under the law of another state.

To the question of whether the United States would follow the lead set by the changes proposed for British law, the answer must be an uncompromising no. This is not only owing to the powers over company law being with the individual states, but much more owing to the power structures within the states and the Federal Government being now in the hands of financial interests which are either linked to company interests or indirectly through the medium of foundations.

To understand the goals of those who wished to change the nature of United States politics and who are still present today, it is necessary to look at the platform of the Libertarian Party for the 1980 Presidential election. "It called for the repeal of all campaign finance laws and the abolition of the Federal Election Commission (FEC). It also favoured the abolition of all government health-care programs, including Medicaid and Medicare. It attacked Social Security as 'virtually bankrupt' and called for its abolition too. Their platform called for the abolition too of the Securities and Exchange Commission, the Environmental Protection Agency, the FBI, and the CIA, amongst other government agencies. It demanded the abolition of 'any laws' impeding employment – by which it meant minimum wage and child labour laws. And it targeted public schools for abolition too, along with what it termed the 'compulsory' education of children ... The platform was, in short, an effort to repeal virtually every major political reform passed during the twentieth century."[89]

I have quoted these objectives at length to illustrate that although the strength of the United States Constitution and

---

[89] Dark Money, Jane Mayer, Scribe 2016.

its courts have severely limited their chance of success, key ones have been achieved, in particular the removal of campaign financing laws, and the scale of overall ambition of sectors of United States society must be kept in mind. The destination has not yet been reached.

When presented in such stark terms, the aims of the Libertarian Party were rejected by the citizens and parties of the United States so that achieving any of the goals required a change of tactic. What this change involved can be seen from comments surrounding the setting-up of a British think-tank following Libertarian ideology, the Institute of Economic Affairs; one of a number of such organisations funded substantially by United States libertarian interests. Taking advice from Hayek, who was at this time teaching at the London School of Economics, one of the founders, quoted by Jane Mayer, wrote that it was "imperative that we give no indication in our literature that we are working to educate the public along certain lines which might be interpreted as having a political bias. In other words, if we said openly that we are re-teaching the economics of the free market, it might enable our enemies to question the charitableness of our motives." This same technique was pursued on a much larger scale across United States academia. By the 1980s, a list of the sponsors of the Heritage Foundation (a free-market think-tank) included Amoco, Amway, Boeing, Chase Manhattan Bank, Chevron, Dow Chemicals, Exxon, General Electric, General Motors, Mesa Petroleum, Mobil Oil, Philip Morris, Proctor & Gamble, R.J. Reynolds, Searl, Sears Roebuck, SmithKline Beecham, Union Carbide, and Union Pacific.

One of the major goals set out by the Libertarian Party was achieved in 2010 when the Supreme Court, in the Citizens United case, lifted all restrictions on company and union spending to elect candidates. Money could not be given directly to candidates – this could be corrupt – but unlimited amounts could be given to independent groups 'technically independent'. Shortly afterwards, the limit on individual spending was lifted and this enabled a part of corporate America to "launch an ambitious, privately financed war of ideas to radically change the country. They didn't want to merely win elections, they wanted to change how Americans thought." (Mayer)

Quoted by Mayer, Phillips-Fein defined the aim in this way "rather than describing the free market as just another economic model, Hayek touted it as the key to all human freedoms. He vilified government as coercive and glorified capitalists as standard bearers for liberty."[90]

By making the price of entry into politics dependent upon vast sums of money, corporate America and its standard-bearers took control of the law-making process and the resulting legislation for their own ends. This process is now so advanced in the United States that any attempt to amend company legislation even slightly in the direction proposed here would be impossible. The United States following a British lead in company law reform is a non-starter.

This fact is understandable in a democracy; the citizens of any democratic country are entitled to define how they wish their laws to influence and affect them. A more pertinent question is whether the United States would accept the proposed changes to United Kingdom company law without taking any action to try to impede or block such developments.

It would be comforting to be able to say that no democratic country would interfere with the internal matters of another democratic country, but the facts contradict this assumption. It is beyond the scope of this book to cover even slightly the scale of United States action in respect of other

---

[90] Kim Phillips-Fein, Invisible Hands, The making of the Conservative Movement from the New Deal to Reagan.

states: this has been done admirably by, amongst others, Naomi Klein in The Shock Doctrine. The mixture of democratic and non-democratic states, either invaded or made the subject of economic sanctions over the last fifty years, for geo-political reasons or at the behest of corporate interests who believe their business has been affected, is extensive. In general, however, western European countries who are also likely to be members of NATO have been spared. This has now ceased to be the case and the most recent handing-down of economic sanctions on the companies of European Union member countries in respect of the Nordstream II project (a 1,234-kilometre-long {767 mile} natural gas pipeline from Russia to Germany running through the Baltic Sea) is yet a new departure for United States intervention in the affairs of friendly, democratic countries. This is both a geo-political and economic matter to the United States, being an attempt to damage Russian gas exports and limit German dependence on Russian gas, and to promote exports of American liquid natural gas, a boost to United States gas-producing companies

This is not difficult to understand since, as most Western politicians recognise but are unwilling to openly acknowledge, the multilateral post-war consensus has broken down. Throughout the 19th century and for the first half of the 20th century, Britain was the world's dominant power, keeping order where it suited and using military power to secure economic dominance. Following the Second World War and the effective bankrupting of Britain coupled with the collapse of the empire, the United States adopted this mantle and spread its economic and military power throughout the non-communist world and, in the face of a perceived threat from communism, this was welcomed by most of the Western world.

The profound changes which occurred in the 1980s and

1990s and which Francis Fukuyama labelled the end of history (The End of History and the Last Man, 1992) were, with hindsight, the beginning of a reversion to the great power politics of the 19th century. Over a short period, the USSR collapsed, almost became a failed state, and then after some recovery tried to enter the capitalist system. China moved towards a capitalist (partly) system, joined the World Trade Organization, and expanded economically. India, the world's biggest democracy, mirrored that expansion. Suddenly powerful, economically and militarily, these countries and others wanted a say in the multilateral bodies and resisted control by the former leaders.

Successive United States governments, seeing the potential loss of hegemony, have been acting behind the scenes to maintain that status but as this has become more difficult this battle has recently become quite open and transparent, leaving the politicians of the US's allies with difficult explanations for their citizens. This development is worrying. China has around 1.6 billion citizens, India around 1.5 billion and the European Union around 450 million, which means they contain roughly 44% of the world's population. It is to be hoped that the United States will find a modus operandi with the rest of the world and not resort to war to try to maintain an unsustainable position in a new post-colonial, post hegemonic world for which the only pattern, not to be followed, is the 19th century. What is most disturbing today is that multilateral bodies, such as the United Nations, the WTO, the International Criminal Court, are not just failing because they are being bypassed or ignored but are actively being attacked and their personnel targeted. This is something new and future generations will not forgive those politicians who remain silent in the face of these attacks.

In my lifetime India, Pakistan, Bangladesh, Vietnam, Cambodia, Laos, Burma, Malaysia, Singapore, Indonesia, Algeria and Sri Lanka, along with almost the whole of Africa and other countries, have emerged from colonialism. Other countries exited 'protectorates' not dissimilar to colonialism, such as Egypt, Libya, and Western powers returned their footholds in countries such as China (Hong Kong). This is not a complete list but informative.

Failing to realise that the world has changed and that some of these countries are economically and militarily strong and, because of their history, will have red lines which it would be unwise to cross may lead to dangerous consequences. Politicians everywhere need a moral compass and a knowledge of recent history to prevent falling into another world war. Einstein was prescient when he said, "I know not with what weapons World War III will be fought, but World War IV will be fought with sticks and stones."

The United States of America has no friends or allies; it has only interests. This has always been true, although concealed from all but astute observers or those affected by this policy. Recently the concealment has ceased, and the full economic power of the country has been directed at supposed ally and foe alike; something which has shocked the West, particularly in Europe who, until now, have been sheltered from this pressure. It is important to remember that, although the West would like to put centuries of colonialism behind it, those countries who were colonised have long memories and will recognise and abhor what they will see as a return to old colonial dominance, in particular when the economic pressure is directed not only at trade but at enforcing political views and action for the US and the countries it supports. With the now almost complete control over politics by corporate interests and the new readiness to act against even friendly democracies, I believe it is almost inconceivable that a reform of British company law along the lines proposed would not elicit from the United States a response, either direct or covert.

Chapter 18
India

India gained independence from the British in 1947, after a long period of colonisation. The economy India inherited was in a backward state; underdeveloped, with low per capita income, poor economic growth, many living below the poverty line, and little industrialisation.

At the time of independence, the Indian Companies Act 1913, as amended by the Indian Companies Bill 1936, which was still in effect, was based on the British Companies Acts 1908 and 1929. The Companies Act 1956, introduced to replace the 1913 Act, was, however, still influenced by the Cohen Commission review of company law in Britain, and the British Companies Act 1948. There were, and still are, relatively close links between United Kingdom company law and that of India.

Because of the scale of underdevelopment, the economic system which was implemented soon after independence included central planning of the economy, the setting up of a large public sector and nationalised banking system, control and licensing of private enterprise, the use of import substituting policies and state control of foreign investment, all implemented largely through the use of statutory legislation.

This led to the conclusion that companies needed to be regulated so that they contributed to economic development rather than being managed in ways that might be viewed as detrimental to the national economic goals. Unlike in Britain, which remained wedded to the 'light touch' concept, the Indian Companies Act 1956 therefore had many provisions which restricted the operations of companies and gave government strong controlling powers. These historic connections can be seen when comparing the Companies Act

2013 of India with Britain's 2006 Act. The relative conservatism of the Indian Act is visible in sections which are more restrictive than similar sections in the British Act but, interestingly, certain sections can be viewed as being in advance of British legislation. Typical of the former, more restrictive sections are those requiring that Indian companies have at least one Indian resident director and have the books of account maintained in India for a minimum of eight years. Equally restrictive but in some ways more forward-thinking are the requirements in respect of independent directors on the boards of listed companies.

The British Companies Act 2006 refers to non-executive directors, who are assumed to be independent, but no definition of 'independent' is supplied. The Indian Act (see Appendix 2) is specific, Section 149 (4) stating: "Every listed public company shall have at least one-third of the total number of directors as independent directors and the Central Government may prescribe the minimum number of independent directors in case of any class or classes of public companies."

Along other, more progressive, lines, the Indian Act stipulates appointment of at least one female director on the board (for a certain class of companies) and also stipulates that certain class of companies must spend a particular amount of money every year on activities/initiatives reflecting Corporate Social Responsibility.

What is a complete diversion from British practice is that legal matters relating to limited companies are dealt with by a National Company Law Tribunal and the National Company Law Appellate Tribunal, which replace the former Company Law Board and Board for Industrial and Financial Reconstruction. These bodies are intended to relieve the Courts of their burden while simultaneously providing specialised justice.

What this brief examination of the similarities and, above

all, the differences between Indian and UK company law, indicates is that it is possible and indeed desirable to write into company law requirements on companies which have a social purpose and limit the possibility of anti-social or damaging actions on the part of companies.

Britain has no foreign direct investment or exchange controls – unlike India which, because of its history and economic position, has maintained strict controls for many years. In 1980, the regulations were relaxed to allow partial participation of foreign capital, but the impact of that relaxation was limited. The Indian Government did not initiate a major change of policy in respect of foreign capital until after the year 2000. A turning point on foreign capital regulation occurred in 2002 when the Indian Government's Department of Commerce changed the one-off approval system for direct investment into a 'negative' system. Industries not on a government list were automatically granted investment approval. In addition, industries such as electric transmission, financial services, and real estate were deregulated in 2005.

Unlike China, which still has a preponderance of state-owned companies, India has an economy primarily driven by private companies. Core among these are multifaceted groups such as Tata, Reliance, and Birla. Tata, as the owner of Jaguar-Land Rover and Tata Steel, has a substantial position in sectors of the British economy. The material difference between Chinese and Indian companies is that those in China often operate through their relationships with government, while those in India are private companies that compete in the market.

India is the second-largest investor in Britain and Britain is the sixth-largest investor in India, the total investment involved being not dissimilar, in the range £25 to £27 billion.

This leads us to the same question which was put in relation to both the United States and China: would a substantial re-writing and tightening on British company law result in a challenge from the Indian Government? I believe not. Indian companies active in Britain may prefer it not to happen, but these companies are reputable and well-run. They can also look to Indian company law and see that there is little cause for complaint.

The Future

Chapter 19
Challenges Still to Come

Two Unavoidable Challenges

There are two serious challenges facing humanity at present and both will inevitably trigger government action; one has been investigated and debated for decades, the other is recent and the direction it will take, and the risks associated with it, are still unclear.

The first is the issue of global climate change, bubbling away beneath the surface for many years, but recent severe weather events and the, by now, obvious changes in the Earth's climate have propelled this challenge to the forefront and have precipitated many international meetings and conferences on this subject. Much more rapid has been the development and ensuing anxiety in respect of artificial intelligence (AI), and the same development will no doubt happen also in the case of AI as governments and global bodies try to grapple with this subject.

Why are these two issues relevant for a book on the limited company? As shown earlier, the limited company is the default legal form for almost all investment in, and control over, the economic factors directing both global climate change and artificial intelligence. In meeting their obligations to their citizens to protect them from the potentially harmful effects of both challenges, governments will have to assume and exercise legal powers which will directly affect the previously presumed autonomy of limited companies in a way unprecedented by past experience.

Of the two risks identified, the more recent – artificial intelligence (AI) – may be the more immediate, although not necessarily the greater, risk.

"The risks of AI systems lie not only in their specific applications but also in the question of who has agency over them at all. At the moment, companies run the show and that is a danger to democracy...

"Any successful AI regulation must tackle three areas. First, the power dynamics between AI developers and the rest of society need rebalancing. This asymmetry is already so significant that only the biggest tech companies can develop AI... as a result, the secrets of AI's inner workings – which have enormous societal impact – remain locked in corporate systems.

"The second problem is access to information. There must be public interest safeguards to allow lawmakers to see the inner workings of AI. There is no public understanding of the algorithms governing apps which affect society. That in turn hinders fact-based discussion, focused public policy, and necessary accountability mechanisms.

"And third, we cannot ignore the ever-changing nature of AI. Regulation needs to be flexible and firmly enforceable. This could include keeping logs so that when settings are adjusted, the impacts can be recorded."[76]

---

[76] Regulating AI will put companies and governments at loggerheads Marietje Schaake May 2 2023
The writer is International Policy Director at Stanford University's Cyber Policy Center and serves as special policy adviser to Margrethe Vestager.
https://www.ft.com/content/7ef4811d-79bb-4b4f-b28f-b46430f0c9ff

The scale of the mismatch between private company expenditure and control over AI has been quantified in a paper by the Massachusetts Institute of Technology in the journal Science. Generative AI needs enormous amounts of data and computing power which, almost exclusively, only large technology companies like Google, Microsoft and Amazon have access to. In 2021, these companies' share of the biggest AI models was 96%. This level of domination is unlikely to change as, also in 2021, non-defence US government agencies allocated $1.5bn to AI. The European Commission planned to spend €1bn on AI in 2021; meanwhile, the private sector invested more than $340bn.

In a leading article, the Editorial Board of the Financial Times put forward two suggestions for inclusion in a regulatory regime which deserves further consideration. One was that algorithms used in critical life-or-death areas, such as healthcare, the judiciary, and the military (I would include education in this list) should be subject to pre-approval in the same way that drugs are approved by monitoring bodies before being made available for use by the public. The second proposal is less radical and, one would hope, would take place in any event. In case of accident, civil aviation authorities can order the suspension from flying of affected aircraft and the introduction of modifications before any further reintroduction of the sanctioned aircraft. It is to be hoped that if a serious and dangerous fault was found in any application of AI which could impact on the citizens, any government would order the immediate cessation of all activity. It would be wise of governments to arm themselves with the legal power to do this in advance, should that be in doubt.

Perhaps the last word in AI should be left to Naomi Klein, author of The Shock Doctrine, and well positioned to comment. She makes the point that for commercial purposes companies are hoovering up vast quantities of data, with or without permission.

"There is a world in which generative AI, as a powerful predictive research tool and a performer of tedious tasks, could indeed be marshalled to benefit humanity, other species and our shared home. But for that to happen, these technologies would need to be deployed inside a vastly different economic and social order than our own, one that had as its purpose the meeting of human needs and the protection of the planetary systems that support all life. Rather, it is built to maximize the extraction of wealth and profit – from both humans and the natural world – a reality that has brought us to what we might think of it as capitalism's techno-necro stage. In that reality of hyper-concentrated power and wealth, AI – far from living up to all those utopian hallucinations – is much more likely to become a fearsome tool of further dispossession and despoilation."[77]

As we have already noted, governments will increasingly have to make difficult decisions in respect of the environment and AI although, with the dangers of global climate change having been identified and measured decades ago, not a great many successful implementation measures can be identified. This is in the nature of genuine global challenges, where some form of global agreement must be reached and then implemented by individual countries or blocks. More is known and more has been tried concerning global climate change, but a brief look at the current position is called for.

The Paris Agreement is a legally binding international treaty on climate change. It was adopted by 196 Parties at

---

[77] AI machines aren't 'hallucinating'. But their makers are. Naomi Klein
Tech CEOs want us to believe that generative AI will benefit humanity. They are kidding themselves
Mon 8 May 2023 09.02 BST
https://www.theguardian.com/commentisfree/2023/may/08/ai-machines-hallucinating-naomi-klein

the UN Climate Change Conference (COP21) in Paris on December 12th 2015. It entered into force on November 4th 2016. Its overarching goal is to hold "the increase in the global average temperature to well below 2°C above pre-industrial levels" and pursue efforts "to limit the temperature increase to 1.5°C above pre-industrial levels" (UNFCCC). To limit global warming to 1.5°C, greenhouse gas emissions must peak before 2025 at the latest and decline 43% by 2030. There is a broad consensus that progress by world governments has been slow. Many commitments have been made but few are binding, and targets are often missed. This is not surprising, as action will often require legislation and the subsequent monitoring of that legislation, and this brings governments, in areas where they are not directly responsible, into potential conflict with companies which control and operate the bulk of assets and activities which generate much of global warming.

In 2019, Britain committed to reach net-zero greenhouse gas emissions by 2050. Since then, it has increased the ambition of its 2030 Nationally Determined Contributions (NDC) to align with this long-term target, aiming to reduce emissions to 68% below 1990 levels by 2030.

It may seem unfair to concentrate on Britain when the problem concerned is a global one, but the governmental problems will be common to all democracies. Britain has, unlike many governments, made substantial commitments towards limiting climate change and overall its record is good compared with many other countries. Despite these efforts, Climate Action Tracker, October 17th 2022, noted:

"The UK's climate action is not consistent with the Paris Agreement. While the UK's NDC and long-term targets are broadly aligned with cost-effective domestic pathways, they do not represent a fair share of the global effort to address climate change. At the moment, under 40% of the emissions reductions required to meet the UK's NDC are supported by policies with proven delivery mechanisms and sufficient funding."

In some areas, Britain has committed to ambitious targets, supported by clear and credible policies including a fully decarbonised power sector by 2035. This is supported by comprehensive policy to drive renewables deployment, including a target of 50GW offshore wind capacity by 2030 and a 2035 ban on fossil-fuelled car sales, supported by a zero-emissions vehicle mandate to drive EV sales in the 2020s. However, UNFCCC also noted areas where the UK lagged, including energy-efficient homes, reducing demand for the most polluting goods and fossil fuel supply, where the government is still approving new oil and gas exploration in the North Sea.

Those areas where the British Government chooses to act and those where it does not act reflect, as in all democracies, the areas where the government of the day has a political interest or sees no threat to it from taking action. Britain is no longer a major car producer; almost all production is foreign-owned, so setting targets is unchallenging. British building companies, which dominate housebuilding, are major contributors to the governing party funds and therefore, perhaps, not to be upset by the setting of severe targets for environmentally friendly housebuilding. By contrast, Germany is probably in the reverse position, as one of the world's leading car producers and exporters, so unwilling to put this position at risk by too stringent legislation and with mainly an owner, occupier building tradition where standards can be set high and mitigating measures taken through tax relief or subsidy.

There is a long history of governments legislating to protect the citizen from dangerous company activity, both unplanned and unforeseen and deliberate. From 19th century labour laws to 20th century legislation banning certain pesticides or legislating for car safety measures, the principle that governments can enforce action or inaction on companies in protection of the citizen is established. What is different in the case of AI and of environmental risk from global climate change is the scale of legislation and interference. One government's action is insufficient and may be negated by the inaction of other governments.

The picture is further clouded by the existence of investor protection clauses in trade treaties which, given the seriousness of the risk facing the world, will have to be watered down or ignored where necessary. Which brings us inevitably to the main requirement on governments in reacting to these global threats: the requirement for transparency, clear signalling of intent, and consistency and fairness in application of the necessary legislation to enforce the measures to limit damage. Supranational bodies, like the European Union, which have traditionally followed this policy (and have the systems in place to carry it out) will lead the way. Britain has not and will struggle; there is no sign of intent or will to change this. This is potentially a recipe for disaster for citizens and for those companies which genuinely wish to contribute and help the world to mitigate these challenges. Those who do not or wish only to benefit financially from the chaos deserve no sympathy. Regretfully, the split is not always clear.

The implementation of the measures proposed in this book coupled with clear laws setting out limits and actions needed to mitigate the effects of both these potentially dangerous developments would go some way to minimise the risks.

Chapter 20
The British Perspective

We have seen that the company was conceived in its present form in the mid-19th century to provide a risk-free home for the large amount of capital available at this time. Parliament was overwhelmed with the demand for statutory companies, which is those created by an act of Parliament, and so an easier alternative was needed

In Britain, at present, a 21st century legal framework is not in place; instead, we have the remnants of the 19th century concept of company law. The 21st century world is a different place and following the horrors of the early half of the 20th century there is, at least in Europe, an understanding and appreciation of the importance of the citizen. In the broad movement towards adult universal suffrage in Britain between 1832 and 1928, it is difficult to discern any impetus given to this struggle by the parallel development of market capitalism, in particular the almost coterminous development of company and mercantile law.

We have seen that United Kingdom company law is predominantly inward-looking, and is concerned with the shareholders, the owners, and to a lesser extent with the creditors of the company. We have noted the limited requirements of the Companies Act 2006 and have seen how relatively little the principles have changed since the inception of modern company law in the 1850s.

Primary control over companies can be exercised by countries through the medium of company legislation and of necessity must be by Britain for both democratic and economic reasons (the two are connected), for the benefit of its citizens. Before we look in more detail at this requirement, we need to examine arguments, already touched on, which could, deliberately or accidentally, lead us up a blind alley.

Is globalisation a threat to Britain? Yes, to some degree, but the threat is much lower than is often perceived. We have seen that world merchandise trade is concentrated into large volumes of exchange between a few major countries or, in the case of the European Union, trade blocks. In comparison with the total British economy, merchandise trade is not large and, as with other large Western economies, is concentrated within a relatively few large companies. This is not true, however, in respect of banking and finance, where Britain has a disproportionately large share of trade in financial 'products'. Because of past failures of the international finance system, this area is monitored and controlled more rigorously than international trade but not as tightly as the citizens of a country such as Britain, exposed to high risk levels, would wish.

If globalisation is not inflicting all or most of the so obvious damage to Britain, what other factor could be in play? Turbo-capitalism, not globalisation, is the main danger and damage factor to privatised social services and to socially necessary public utilities such as power and water in Britain, resulting from a combination of weak company law and a belief that weakly regulated competition is the road to economic success (despite decades of evidence to the contrary, successive British governments have clung to this fallacy).

Another potential blind alley is the argument that the 'markets' control policy, and that governments are helpless in the face of corporate pressure. Political parties and politicians vacillate in respect of the power of the market; sometimes it is dominant and cannot be challenged, and at other times governments simply pass laws or issue edicts at short notice, or even overnight, to close or limit markets or prohibit companies from carrying out activities they have previously carried out quite legally. Often this is done citing security concerns, sometimes real and sometimes economically convenient but rarely in the name of protecting the health or economic wellbeing of their own citizens or those of other countries. Clearly governments have huge, in some cases unlimited, power over market participants, including companies, and the decision as to whether they choose to use it is a political decision, often led by ideology or regulatory capture.

Now that we accept that governments, including British governments, have the power to regulate companies in the interest of their citizens, what needs to be done? The whole concept of the 'limited liability company' has been distorted, particularly in the last forty years, to the advantage of a small section of society and the detriment of the vast majority. This distortion must be reversed.

Most companies, large and small, are owned and managed by socially responsible citizens; they will not be disturbed or affected by these changes. Only a small but probably vociferous, influential and damaging minority will be unhappy. Capitalism is both constructive and destructive and will remain so. The only relevant question is, during its destructive phase who suffers the consequences? Presently it is chiefly society and the citizen, and only by changing the rules at the level of legislation can this trend be reversed.

There is no need to repeat in detail the proposals for updating British company law, but a brief reminder of the main points may be helpful. The two most important legal changes needed would completely ban companies from all political activity and from the funding of political parties, under the threat of severe penalties. Added would be the requirement for complete transparency in all interaction with government, excluding of course any with a national security element. That this can be achieved is shown by the way the European Union publishes on its websites details even of trade negotiations with other countries, a benefit to the citizen which led to the ending of trade negotiations with the United States when the nature of the potential agreement was understood. Much of what is considered to be of a national security nature is simply to avoid embarrassment to a government or to ensure an unpopular measure is passed.

The other material changes to be introduced include subjecting companies to all laws, removing limited liability from subsidiaries, creating transparent and demanding company forms for social and infrastructure companies, and requiring adequate levels of maintained capitalisation in companies. It is obvious that the payment of fair and proportionate tax with the closure of current loopholes is required, and that management must be made responsible for achieving these ends, with proportionate levels of punishment for deliberate or overtly careless failure.

A new 'Golden Age' like the one which occurred at the turn of the 19th century, where capital amassed enormous wealth, has repeated itself at the turn of the 20th century. Finance is in control and its instrument is the limited liability company. This has not gone unnoticed, but what has been ignored is that the solution is on hand in the form of primary company legislation to ensure that this instrument works for the citizen, not against them.

Chapter 21
Where to Now?

It is possible to become demotivated by the repeated description of economic damage, eloquently and exhaustively set out by academic writers and journalists but without any proposals for a solution; perhaps because the obvious solution is controversial and politically demanding. Secondary monitoring with weak, underfunded bodies has never succeeded. The financial press provides a good idea of the world of geo-politics better, throwing light on the huge flow of funds and assets moving around the world under the control mainly of companies, worsened by the recent outbreak of wars, often with the co-operation and/or encouragement of politicians. The world is awash with money, in the hands of companies, hedge funds, private equity companies and individuals. Unfortunately not enough of it is available to governments to meet the requirements of the citizen.

The key lies with company law but despite its potential, if radically redrawn in favour of the citizen, to limit the excesses of turbo-capitalism and its potential to damage society, it is in most countries the least examined and discussed area of law.

Few philosophers of political economy have looked in detail at the company; most analysis and comment has been by legal theorists and economic historians. Marx and Engels can be excused; they wrote when the company was not yet the norm, but later writers appear not to have recognised the significance of the explosion in companies and their influence economically and politically or, when they have, hoped that multilateral bodies would provide the necessary control. Rawls concentrated on the justice and fairness of the state, whilst recognising that his approach could be employed for major sub-structures created by the state. Right-wing philosophers such as Robert Nozick (best known for his defence of libertarianism in his Anarchy, State and Utopia (1974)) concentrated on defending property rights after all other powers of the state, except for the maintenance of law and order, had been removed. Had Nozick been compelled to examine in detail the company in its present form, I am convinced that he would have had to reject the concept as an interference by the state which both enabled and encouraged fraud (otherwise why the auditor and extensive regulation?) and that the true libertarian would trade without limited liability and stand behind his or her transactions with all their assets.

The political battle today in the Western democracies is not between communism and fascism or between socialism and capitalism but between a world as envisioned by Rawls and one as proposed by Nozick. The forces behind the Nozick view have made and continue to make gains in the West and the first step in halting this advance should begin by redrafting the law governing the company, to spell out in detail the responsibilities of management and the penalties for breaching these, and to tighten the capital requirements and narrow the tax avoidance possibilities so that the company functions also for the individual citizen and society.

Setting out the history of the company and its resulting damage is important since today the current position is again at risk and we are once again seeing the rise of a management philosophy which improves results by slashing research and development, training and investment, chiefly because of the often excessive leverage incurred in buying companies effectively with their own money, borrowing huge sums which together with interest must be repaid by extracting cash from the target company, often at the expense of the key elements of company success. This process was damaging when for a prolonged period interest rates were almost zero but as rates return to a more normal level the strains of this model can destroy otherwise healthy companies. We have come full circle.

The damage in the 1970s and 1980s was the result of greed and ignorance (amplified through thousands of business school MBAs) but today we can exclude ignorance, leaving only greed and a disregard for the long-term financial health of key companies and social nets and for the welfare of the citizen.

This is hugely damaging to society as consciously or subconsciously citizens see these changes taking place and this, coupled with falling income levels for substantial numbers of citizens and the rapid and transparent decline in public services, leads inevitably to a feeling of alienation and helplessness. This also presents a gift to the politician who chooses to direct this alienation into hatred of the other, such as immigrants or ethnic minorities, and who offers a simple solution to what is a complex issue unrelated to the suggested cause. The power of companies, even multinational groups, is within states' control; states remain the global power actors. Corporate social responsibility gives too much credence to the company and is a distraction from more direct and effective action.

Is there any evidence that managers have learned from the excesses that have been the cause of repeated crises? The philosophy of 'shareholder value' has corrupted any previously held principles of social solidarity on the part of managers and has been replaced by a philosophy intent on increasing profits in the shortest possible time, often by any means possible. The company becomes nothing more than a profit-generating unit within which anything and everyone is open to replacement if they do not serve that aim.

The key point to make is that the tool to change the nature of turbo-capitalism as distinct from globalisation, which represents a different challenge, is company law.

Globalisation, limited in scale, is a neutral concept and need not always be negative. We have already seen that some major multi-national companies have kept the social contract with their own citizens, whilst creating jobs and knowledge in less developed countries, whilst others have not and have simply followed low-cost employment opportunities.

Turbo-capitalism, by contrast, often uses the assets which we all need as humans in the modern world, such as water, power, raw materials, social services, commodities and even food as chips in a huge game of chance, uninterested in any damage it may cause to their fellow citizens.

A New Act

A radical redrafting of the Companies Act 2006 will be a challenge both in principle and in detail for legal minds, less for what needs to be added but more in respect of what needs removing or shortening. The Act is the largest piece of legislation ever passed by Parliament, with 1300 sections, sixteen schedules, and runs to around 760 pages. It is overwhelmingly inward-looking, concerned with the technical running of companies and not their interaction with the state, the citizen or society. The twelve sections and approximately six pages on the General Duties of Directors is little more than exhortation, whereas the thirty-five sections and about seventeen pages on Resolutions at Meeting go into painstaking detail, as do the fifty-five sections and approximately twenty-four pages on Appointment of Auditors.

Recent British corporate history shows that this massive

legislation has singularly failed in its intended purpose, to control the internal management of companies and their overview, so that serious simplification can scarcely do any further damage. More important is the extending of the legislation to those important political, social, and environmental areas which it does not yet cover. In drafting new legislation, the starting point will need to be the overall aim of the legislation, particularly those key protections which are not currently included. That this can be achieved is illustrated by the setting-up of the NHS in 1948 where, despite being faced with other challenges, government decided on its grand aim and key objectives and the legislation speedily followed. Put simply, there is no other practical way of taming turbo-capitalism as weak monitoring and codes of conduct have failed.

Politicians can demand that action be taken and changes implemented following which civil servants and lawyers can produce the necessary legislation. It is that easy! And that legislation should be extensive and inclusive, to reduce the need for the currently ineffectual monitoring bodies which continue to proliferate in the UK.

Marxist historians may well argue that it is the concept of the limited liability company which is the cause of all problems, and some may go so far as to suggest its abolition, but the radical rewriting of company law with the citizen in mind will benefit society and the individual citizen, particularly if that rewrite is so radical that sufficient of the corporate veil is removed to ensure transparency and fiscal probity for the benefit of all. One of the biggest challenges facing a new company law, after banning all political activity and financing, will be to constrain the concept of commercial confidentiality to those cases where it may apply and ending it where the state is involved, or where activity is conducted on behalf of the state.

One of the most damaging effects of placing a company operating commercially in the position of carrying out social functions is that employees are then heavily constrained legally from expressing moral outrage or exposing wrongdoing. Their duty is to their employer and not their fellow citizens. This also gives powers to management, unelected and answerable only, in theory, to their shareholders, to monitor and control their fellow citizens, and as such is profoundly undemocratic. A company can be justified in this situation only when the citizen can choose whether to use its services or not.

How this can be assessed and justified is best done by avoiding Britain's traditional philosophical fallback of relying on utilitarian principles and by embracing the concepts of justice and fairness as set out by Rawls and dealing with each point of principle individually from the viewpoint of the informed citizen. There can be an instinctive anti-intellectual streak in Britain which espouses to despise a philosophical approach (unless, currently, proposed by right-wing American writers) but which is based on a fear of engaging with challenging ideas based on principle and justice.

Capitalism has failure built into it, it is inevitable. The question is as to who picks up the cost following the failure. It is simply necessary to define the parameters within which they may do so and set the penalties for breaching those rules. Ensuring that companies contribute adequately to society's costs by closing methods of tax evasion efficiently and effectively does not prevent them from investing and developing their business, nor should the cost of any measures be a hindrance as they will be self-financing given the current level of evasion.

In a freedom of information request, HMRC disclosed that British residents in 2019 had £850 billion in accounts overseas, of which £570 was in tax havens, but they were unable to say what proportion of this had been correctly disclosed.

Taking a stance on this will mean challenging the status quo not just at home but in the wider world: the company, its existence, treatment and encouragement is one of the few values that the US, UK, the EU, China and India have in common. Which UK politician and which political party will have the courage to do this, and act in the interest of the citizens of the UK?

Appendix 1
Companies Act 1862

The format and content of the 1862 Act would be readily recognisable to the reader of later United Kingdom companies acts and although there is always a risk of overloading readers with too much detail, it will be useful for the non-specialist reader to have a broad overview of the key parts of the 1862 Act, as these concepts are constant for the next 150 years up to and including the 2006 Act. As noted in the preliminary preamble to the Act, it is divided into nine parts, of which the first five are the most relevant.

The first part refers to the "constitution and incorporation of companies and associations under this Act". (Sections 6-21).

The Act allows any seven or more persons to subscribe to a Memorandum of Association which sets out the proposed structure of the company, including the capital structure and the form of limited liability. One requirement in the Memorandum is to set out the objects of the company, that is, for what purpose was the company formed. This requirement remained in force for a considerable time before eventually being abandoned. We will look at this again. For a company limited by shares, that is most companies, the Memorandum, when filed with the Registrar of Companies, may also be accompanied by the Articles of Association setting out the regulations for the internal running of the company. The Act's drafters helpfully included draft Articles of Association under Table A of Schedule One to the Act.

The second part of the Act relates to the "distribution of the capital and liabilities of members of companies and associations under this Act." (Sections 22-38). The Act requires every company to keep a register of members at its registered office and supply this once a year to the Registrar of Joint Stock Companies.

The third part of the Act covers "management and administration of companies and associations" (Sections 39-73). This section covers many of the key requirements on the company in respect of creditors. All companies must keep an identified registered office for the receipt of legal notices and companies must identify themselves with the word 'Limited' in their title. All limited companies must keep a publicly accessible register of all mortgages and charges affecting the property of the company along with a register of the directors and managers of the company. For the protection of members, a General Meeting is to be held at least once every year and details outlining the process and requirements for passing a special resolution. Section 56 gives the Board of Trade the powers to appoint inspectors to examine the affairs of any company under the Act with details of the powers of inspectors. By special resolution, the company itself could also appoint inspectors to report to the General Meeting.

The longest part of the Act is Part Four, relating to the winding-up of companies. One reason for the length of this section is the requirement at this time to cover legal issues in England, Scotland and Ireland so that the same section is repeated under the requirements of each jurisdiction. The English court system was also somewhat different and required more extensive narration as to enforcement. Subject to these caveats, the basic structure of winding up a company under United Kingdom company law is set out in this act. Companies may be wound up either by the court or voluntarily. The substantive reasons for winding up are either that the company has passed a special resolution requiring the company to be wound up by the court or that the company is unable to pay its debts. An inability to meet a demand by a creditor within three weeks could lead to a court ordering the winding up of a company.

Official Liquidator(s) are to be appointed by the court and although their powers and duties are set out in detail in the Act, the court has power to amend them as well as the power to order the collection and application of assets. When the affairs of the company are wound up, the court will order the dissolution of the company. There was certainly no strong feeling at this point that companies should be kept 'alive'; they are there for a purpose and that purpose had failed. The assets will not disappear and can be re-purposed; only the legal fiction – the name on a piece of paper – disappears. The court has extraordinary powers to summon anyone suspected of holding assets of the company, to examine them under oath, and to empower the liquidator to order their arrest if there is any fear of them absconding.

The Act also foresees voluntary winding up of a company. A voluntary winding-up assumes that a company is solvent and requires a liquidator to be appointed to wind up the affairs of the company and distribute its property. A court could also direct that a voluntary winding-up be subject to court supervision. The 1862 Act is much more direct than today in respect of misfeasance with the ability of the court to assess damages against 'delinquent' directors and officers and sets out severe penalties for the falsification of the books and records of the companies, with a penalty of "imprisonment for any term not exceeding two years with or without hard labour".

Part Five of the act is concerned with the setting up and constitution of the Registration Office whilst Part Six concerns the application of the Act to companies formed under the Joint Stock Companies Acts. Part Seven covers the regulations as to the registration of existing companies, Part Eight with the winding up of unregistered companies and Part Nine with the repeal of earlier acts.

This outline was to remain broadly unchanged into the future.

The introduction of the holding company – that is, the ability of one company to own another – led directly to today's multi-national groups, but at no stage of this development is it possible to identify any plan or strategic overview. On the contrary, these developments were unconnected and almost accidental, with no interest on their likely effect on society or the state.

The 1862 act led to, if not an explosion, certainly a rapid acceleration in the formation of new companies, in particular financial companies, and may well have precipitated the banking crisis of 1866. This rapid expansion, subsequent financial collapse, and the legal decisions which the courts were then forced to make, quickly led to a series of unintended consequences with which we are still living today..

The sheer volume of capital available at this time is best illustrated by the formation of companies and most significantly the level of their capitalisation. From the returns for 1862 presented to Parliament in 1863, there were 422 companies formed in England in that year, along with thirty-eight banks. The smallest company was the Bakers Free Press and General Advertiser Newspaper, with an authorised capital of £200 with £173.15 paid-up (£10,000 as a modern-day equivalent of the 1856 value) and the largest the United Mexican Mining Company Ltd with an issued and paid capital of £1,295,220 (equivalent £74,000,000). The average issued and almost completely paid-up capital of the 422 companies was £66,130 (equivalent £3,770,000) and for the thirty-eight banks it was

£893,000 (equivalent £51,000,000). Clearly the least concern of legislators in 1856 was the level of limited liability company capitalisation.

Appendix 2
Companies Act India, Section 149

(4) Every listed public company shall have at least one-third of the total number of directors as independent directors and the Central Government may prescribe the minimum number of independent directors in case of any class or classes of public companies.

Explanation. --For the purposes of this sub-section, any fraction contained in such one-third number shall be rounded off as one.

(5) Every company existing on or before the date of commencement of this Act shall, within one year from such commencement or from the date of notification of the rules in this regard as may be applicable, comply with the requirements of the provisions of sub-section (4).

(6) An independent director in relation to a company, means a director other than a managing director or a whole-time director or a nominee director, --

(a) who, in the opinion of the Board, is a person of integrity and possesses relevant expertise and experience.

(b) (i) who is or was not a promoter of the company or its holding, subsidiary or associate company.

(ii) who is not related to promoters or directors in the company, its holding, subsidiary or associate company.

(c) who has or had no pecuniary relationship with the company, its holding, subsidiary or associate company, or their promoters, or directors, during the two immediately preceding financial years or during the current financial year.

(d) none of whose relatives has or had pecuniary relationship or transaction with the company, its holding, subsidiary or associate company, or their promoters, or directors, amounting to two per cent or more of its gross turnover or total income or fifty lakh rupees or such higher amount as may be prescribed, whichever is lower, during the two immediately preceding financial years or during the current financial year.

(e) who, neither himself nor any of his relatives--

(i) holds or has held the position of a key managerial personnel or is or has been employee of the company or its holding, subsidiary or associate company in any of the three financial years immediately preceding the financial year in which he is proposed to be appointed.

(ii) is or has been an employee or proprietor or a partner, in any of the three financial years immediately preceding the financial year in which he is proposed to be appointed.

Glossary

AI. Artificial Intelligence.
A field of study in computer science that develops and studies intelligent machines and software.

ACUE. American Committee for a United Europe.
A committee set up by US politicians after the Second World War, at the instigation of UK politicians, to fund the European Movement, a supporter of European union.

Aktiengesellschaft (AG).
German Public Limited Company.

Bill of Lading.
A legal document issued by a carrier to a shipper which details the goods being carried. A bill of lading is a document of title, a receipt for shipped goods, and a contract between a carrier and a shipper.

BoE. Bank of England.
The central bank of the UK tasked with maintaining monetary and financial stability.

EEC. European Economic Community.
Predecessor to the European Union created in 1957 by the Treaty of Rome.

EU. European Union.
A European supranational political and economic union of 27 member states.

FCA. Financial Conduct Authority.
The conduct regulator for financial services firms and financial markets in the UK.

G20. Group of 20.
An intergovernmental forum comprising 19 sovereign countries, the European Union (EU), and the African Union (AU).

GATT. The General Agreement on Tariffs and Trade
Signed in 1947, it was a treaty minimizing barriers to international trade by eliminating or reducing quotas, tariffs, and subsidies. Succeeded by the World Trade Organization.

Forex. A foreign currency futures contract.
An agreement between two parties to deliver a set amount of currency at a set date in the future.

Gesellschaft mit beschrankter Haftung. GmbH.
German Private Limited Company.

ISDS. Investor–State Dispute Settlement
A set of rules through which countries can be sued by foreign investors.

IMF. The International Monetary Fund.
A major financial agency of the United Nations and the global lender of last resort to national governments.

Legal identity.
Formally incorporated organisations have their own legal identity, and can hold assets, enter contracts and be sued in their own name.

Letter of Comfort.
A written document that provides a level of assurance that an obligation will ultimately be met. It may not be legally enforceable.

Limited Liability Company.
A private company whose owners are legally responsible for its debts only to the extent of the amount of capital they have invested.

NBFI. Non-banking Financial Institution.
A financial institution that does not have a full banking license and cannot accept deposits from the public.

OECD. The Organization for Economic Cooperation and Development.
Works to establish evidence-based international standards and solutions to a range of social, economic and environmental challenges.

PLC. Public Limited Company.
Offers shares to the general public either privately by an Initial Public Offering (IPO) or by trades on the stock market.

PRA. Prudential Regulation Authority.
Part of the Bank of England. Supervises financial institutions including banks and insurance companies.

PuSC. A Community Interest Company.
A special type of limited company which exists to benefit the community rather than private shareholders and with an 'asset lock'; a legal promise stating that the company's assets will only be used for its social objectives.

Private Limited Company.
Private companies may issue stock and have shareholders, but their shares do not trade on public exchanges and are not issued through an IPO.

SOE
State-owned enterprise.

SWIFT. The Society for Worldwide Interbank Financial Telecommunication.
A Belgian banking cooperative providing services for the execution of financial transactions and payments between limited banks worldwide.

TRIPS. The Agreement on Trade-Related Aspects of Intellectual Property Rights.
An international legal agreement between all the member nations of the World Trade Organization to protect intellectual property rights.

UNFCCC. United Nations Framework Convention on Climate Change.
Aimed at preventing "dangerous" human interference with the climate system.

Ultra Vires. Literally translated as "beyond the powers".
Used to describe an act which requires legal authority or power but is then completed outside of or without the requisite authority.

WTO. The World Trade Organization.
A global international organization dealing with the rules of trade between nations. Unlike its predecessor GATT (see above) it has, in theory, enforcement mechanisms.

Bibliography

2011. Derivatives: A Twenty-First Century Understanding, Timothy E Lynch

A Theory of Justice, John Rawls (Harvard, 1971)

An Introduction to the Principles of Morals and Legislation, Jeremy Bentham, 1780

Anarchy, State and Utopia, Robert Nozick, (Wiley-Blackwell, 2013) ISBN 978-0465051007

Breaking the WTO, Kristen Hopewell (Stanford University Press, 2016)

Capitalism's Victor's Justice? The Hidden Stories Behind the Prosecution of Industrialists Post-WWII, Grietje Baars. (OUP)

Companies Act India 2013

Company Law in China, Jiangyu Wang, Edward Elgar. 2014, 9781849805728

Danni Rodrik, Journal of Economic Perspectives

Dark Money, Jane Mayer (Scribe)

David Foucaud in Revue économique Volume 62, Issue 5, 2011, pages 867 to 897

Democracy For Sale, Peter Geoghegan, (Head Zeus, 2020) ISBN (PB) 9781789546040

Germany, Aktiengesetz and GmbHG

Hitler's Cartel, Diarmuid Jeffreys (Bloomsbury Publishing, 2008)

Limited Liability and Corporate Groups, Phillip Blumberg (University of Connecticut Law School, 1986)

Limited Liability and the Modern Corporation in Theory and Practice, Stephanie Blankenburg, Dan Plesch and Frank Wilkinson (Cambridge Journal of Economics, 2010, 34, 821-836)

MA Thesis, Robert Simon Yavner (Old Dominion University, August 1984)

Multinational Enterprises and the Law, Peter T Muchlinski, (The Oxford International Law Library), ISBN 978-0-19-922797-9

National Corporate Law in a Globalised Market, David Milman (Edward Elgar, 2009)

Red Capitalism, Carl E Walter and Fraser J T H Howie, (Wiley, 2012) ISBN 9781118255100 (hb)

The Age of Surveillance Capitalism, Shoshana Zuboff, Profile Books Ltd., ISBN 9781781256855

The Almighty Dollar, Dharshini David (Elliot and Thompson Ltd)

The Brussels Effect, Anu Bradford, (Oxford University Press), ISBN 9780190088583 (HB)

The Collapse of Globalism, John Ralston Saul, (Atlantic Books, 2005) London, CIP 1843544091

The Companies Act, 1862, Anthony Pulbrook, (Leopold Classic Library, 2015)

The Companies Acts UK, 1855, 1862, 1908, 1928, 1948, 1967, 1981, 1985, 1989, 2006

The Company, John Micklethwaite and Adrian Wooldridge (Phoenix, 2003)

The Corporation, Joel Bakan (Constable, 2004)

The Emergence of Private Authority in Global Governance, Rodney Bruce Hall and Thomas Biersteker(eds) (Cambridge University Press, 2002)

The Failure of Corporate Law, Kent Greenfield, (University of Chicago Press, 2006)

The Finance Curse, Nicholas Shaxson, (The Bodley Head, London, 2018) ISBN 9781847925381(hb)

The Globalisation Paradox, Dani Rodrik, (Oxford University Press, 2011) ISBN 987-0-19-965252-5 (pbk)

The ICSA Companies Act 2006 Handbook, 2nd Edition, Consultant Editor Keith Walmsley

The Politics of Jurisprudence, Roger Cotterrell (University of Pennsylvania Press, 1989)

The Price of Inequality, Joseph E Stiglitz (Penguin, 2012)

The Silent Takeover, Noreena Hertz (Heinemann, 2001)

Victorian People. Asa Briggs, (Penguin Books,1953,1977)
Volume 32, number 2 - Spring 2018 Pages 73 -9